CAMBRIDGE LIBRARY COLLECTION

Books of enduring scholarly value

Literary Studies

This series provides a high-quality selection of early printings of literary works, textual editions, anthologies and literary criticism which are of lasting scholarly interest. Ranging from Old English to Shakespeare to early twentieth-century work from around the world, these books offer a valuable resource for scholars in reception history, textual editing, and literary studies.

Double Falshood, or, The Distrest Lovers

Double Falshood was staged at the Theatre Royal in Drury Lane at the end of 1727, and the following year Lewis Theobald (1688–1744) published the text, which was reprinted several times. Theobald was an energetic editor who translated Sophocles' *Electra* and Aristophanes' *Plutus* for performance in London, wrote and edited many other dramatic works, and caused great controversy in literary circles with his *Shakespeare Restored* (1726), a critique of Pope's edition. Scholars have debated for nearly three centuries to what extent, if at all, *Double Falshood* derives from a lost play by Shakespeare, as Theobald claimed. There is now widespread agreement that it is the only surviving version of Shakespeare and Fletcher's *Cardenio*, which was based on episodes from Cervantes' *Don Quixote* and is known to have been performed in 1613. Interest generated by the play's partial acceptance into the Shakespearean canon has also led to modern revivals.

T0352311

Double Falshood

or, The Distrest Lovers

*A Play, as it is Acted at the
Theatre-Royal in Drury-Lane*

Written Originally by
W. Shakespeare

Edited by Lewis Theobald

CAMBRIDGE UNIVERSITY PRESS

Cambridge, New York, Melbourne, Madrid, Cape Town,
Singapore, São Paolo, Delhi, Mexico City

Published in the United States of America by Cambridge University Press, New York

www.cambridge.org
Information on this title: www.cambridge.org/9781108019521

This edition first published 1728
This digitally printed version 2012

ISBN 978-1-108-01952-1 Paperback

Double Falſhood;

O R,

The DISTREST LOVERS.

A

[*Price* 1 *s. and* 6 *d.*]

G E O R G E R.

 EORGE the Second, by the Grace of God, King of *Great-Britain, France* and *Ireland*; Defender of the Faith, *&c.* To all to whom thefe Prefents fhall come, Greeting. Whereas our Trufty, and Well-beloved *Lewis Theobald,* of our City of *London,* Gent. hath, by his Petition, humbly reprefented to Us, That He having, at a confiderable Expence, Purchafed the Manufcript Copy of an Original Play of WILLIAM SHAKESPEARE, called, *Double Falfhood*; *Or, the Diftreft Lovers*; and, with great Labour and Pains, Revifed, and Adapted the fame to the Stage; has humbly befought Us, to grant him Our Royal Privilege, and Licence, for the fole Printing and Publifhing thereof, for the Term of Fourteen Years: We, being willing to give all due Encouragement to this his Undertaking, are gracioufly pleafed to condefcend to his Requeft: and do therefore, by thefe Prefents, fo far as may be agreeable to the Statute in that Behalf made and provided, for Us, Our Heirs, and Succeffors, grant unto Him, the faid *Lewis Theobald,* his Executors, Adminiftrators, and Affigns, Our Royal Licence, for the fole Printing and Publifhing the faid Play, in fuch Size and Manner, as He and They fhall think fit, for the Term of Fourteen Years, to be computed from the Date hereof; ftrictly forbidding all our Subjects within our Kingdoms and Dominions, to Reprint the fame, either in the like, or in any other Size, or Manner whatfoever; or to Import, Ruy, Vend, Utter or Diftribute any Copies thereof, Reprinted beyond the Seas, during the aforefaid Term of Fourteen Years, without the Confent, or Approbation of the faid *Lewis Theobald,* his Heirs, Executors, and Affigns, under his, or their Hands and Seals firft had, and obtained; as they will anfwer the contrary at their Peril: —— Whereof the Commiffioners, and other Officers of our Cuftoms, the Mafter, Warden, and Company of Stationers, are to take Notice, that the fame may be entred in the Regifter of the faid Company, and that due Obedience be rendred thereunto. Given at Our Court at St. *James's,* the Fifth Day of *December,* 1727; in the Firft Year of Our Reign.

By His Majefty's Command,

HOLLES NEWCASTLE.

Double Falfhood;

O R,

The DISTREST LOVERS.

A

P L A Y,

As it is Acted at the

THEATRE-ROYAL

I N

D R U R T-L A N E.

Written Originally by *W. SHAKESPEARE*;
And now Revifed and Adapted to the Stage
By Mr. Theobald, the Author of *Shakefpeare Reftor'd.*

—— *Quod optanti Divûm promittere nemo*
Auderet, volvenda Dies, en! attulit ultrò.   Virg.

L O N D O N:

Printed by J. Watts, at the Printing-Office in
Wild-Court near *Lincolns-Inn Fields.*

M DCC XXVIII.

To the Right HONOURABLE

George Dodington, Efq;

S I R,

OTHING can more ftrongly fecond the Pleafure I feel, from the Univerfal Applaufe which crowns this *Orphan* Play, than this Other which I take in prefuming to fhelter it under Your Name. I bear fo dear an Affection to the Writings and Memory of SHAKESPEARE, that, as it is my good Fortune to retrieve this Remnant of his Pen from Obfcurity, fo it is my greateft Ambition that

A 3   this

DEDICATION.

this Piece fhould be received into the Protection of fuch a Patron: And, I hope, Future Times, when they mean to pay *Shakefpeare* the beft Compliment, will remember to fay, Mr. DODINGTON was that Friend to his *Remains*, which his own SOUTHAMPTON was to his *living Merit*.

It is from the *fine Difcernment* of our Patrons, that we can generally beft promife Ourfelves the good Opinion of the Publick. You are not only a diftinguifh'd *Friend* of the *Mufes*, but moft intimately *allied* to them: And from hence it is I flatter Myfelf, that if You fhall think fit to pronounce this Piece genuine, it will filence the Cenfures of thofe *Unbelievers*, who think it impoffible a

Ma-

DEDICATION.

Manufcript of *Shakefpeare* could fo
long have lain dormant; and who
are blindly paying Me a greater
Compliment than either They defign, or I can merit, while they care
not but confefs Themfelves *pleafed,*
yet would fain infinuate that they
are *impofed upon.* I fhould efteem it
fome Sort of *Virtue,* were I able to
commit fo *agreeable* a *Cheat.*

But pardon Me, Sir, for a Di-
greffion that perverts the very Rule
of Dedications. I own, I have my
Reafons for it. As, SIR, your
known Integrity, and Honour en-
gages the warmeft Wifhes of all good
Men for your Profperity, fo your
known Diftinction in polite Letters,
and your generous Encouragement
of Thofe who pretend to them, o-
bliges us to confider your Advance-

ment

DEDICATION.

ment, as our own perfonal Intereſt, and as a good Omen, at leaſt, if not as the ſureſt Means of the future flouriſhing Condition of thoſe *Humane* Arts amongſt us, which We *profeſs*, and which You *adorn*. But neither Your Modeſty, nor my Inability will ſuffer me to enter upon that Subject. Permit me therefore, SIR, to convert *Panegyrick* into a moſt ardent Wiſh, that You would look with a Tender Eye on this *dear Relick*, and that you would believe me, with the moſt unfeigned Zeal and Reſpect,

SIR,

Your moſt Devoted

and Obedient Humble Servant,

Great Ruſſell-ſtreet,
21*ſt* December,
1727.

LEW. THEOBALD.

PREFACE

OF THE

EDITOR.

T HE Succefs, which this Play has met with from the Town in the Reprefentation, (to fay nothing of the Reception it found from thofe Great Judges, to whom I have had the Honour of communicating it in Manufcript;) has almoft made the Purpofe of a Preface unneceffary : And therefore what I have to fay, is defign'd rather to wipe out a flying Objection ro two, than to labour at proving it the Production of *Shake-fpeare*. It has been alledg'd as incredible, that fuch a Curiofity fhould be ftifled and loft to the World for above a Century. To This my Anfwer is fhort; that tho' it never till now made its Appearance on the Stage, yet one of the Manufcript Copies, which I have, is of above Sixty Years Standing, in the Handwriting of Mr. *Downes*, the famous Old Prompter; and, as I am credibly inform'd, was early in the Poffeffion of the celebrated Mr. *Betterton*, and by Him defign'd to have been ufher'd into the World. What Accident prevented This Purpofe of his, I do not pretend to know: Or thro' what hands it had fucceffively pafs'd before that Period of Time. There is a Tradition (which I have from the Noble Perfon, who fupply'd me with One of my Copies) that it was given by our Author, as a Prefent of Value, to a Natural Daughter of his, for whofe Sake he wrote it, in the Time of his Retirement from the Stage. Two other Copies I have, (one of which I was glad to purchafe

PREFACE.

chafe at a very good Rate,) which may not, perhaps, be quite fo Old as the Former; but One of Them is much more perfect, and has fewer Flaws and Interruptions in the Senfe.

Another Objection has been ftarted, (which would carry much more Weight with it, were it Fact;) that the Tale of this Play, being built upon a Novel in *Don Quixot*, Chronology is againft Us, and *Shakefpeare* could not be the Author. But it happens, that *Don Quixot* was publifh'd in the Year 1611, and *Shake-fpeare* did not dye till *April* 1616, a fufficient Interval of Time for All that We want granted.

Others again, to depreciate the Affair, as they thought, have been pleafed to urge, that tho' the Play may have fome Refem-blances of *Shakefpeare*, yet the *Colouring*, *Diction*, and *Chara-cters*, come nearer to the Style and Manner of FLETCHER. This, I think, is far from deferving any Anfwer; I fubmit it to the Determination of better Judgments; tho' my Partiality for *Shakefpeare* makes me wifh, that Every Thing which is good, or pleafing, in our Tongue, had been owing to his Pen.

As to the Performance of the refpective *Actors* concern'd in this Play, my applauding It here would be altogether fuper-fluous. The Publick has diftinguifh'd and given them a Praife, much beyond Any that can flow from my Pen. But I have fome particular Acknowledgments to make to the *Managers* of this Company, for which I am glad to embrace fo fair an Op-portunity.

I came to Them at this Juncture as an *Editor*, not an *Au-thor*, and have met with fo much Candour, and handfome Treatment from Them, that I am willing to believe, the Complaint, which has fo commonly obtain'd, of their Difre-gard and ill Behaviour to Writers, has been more feverely urg'd, than it is juftly grounded. They muft certainly be too good Judges of their own Intereft, not to know that a Theatre cannot always fubfift on old Stock, but that the Town requires Novelty at their Hands. On the other Hand, they muft be fo far Judges of their own Art and Profeffion, as to know that all the Compofitions, which are offer'd them, would never go down with Audiences of fo nice and deli-cate a Tafte, as in this Age frequent the Theatres. It would be very hard upon fuch a Community, where fo many Interefts are concern'd, and fo much Merit in their Bufi-nefs allow'd, if they had not a Priviledge of refufing fome crude Pieces, too imperfect for the Entertainment of the Pub-lick I would not be thought to inferr, that they have ne-ver difcourag'd what They might, perhaps, afterwards wifh they had receiv'd. They do not, I believe, fet up for fuch a Conftant

PREFACE.

ſtant Infallibility. But if We do but fairly conſider out of a-
bove Four Thouſand Plays extant, how ſmall a Number will
now ſtand the Teſt: if We do but conſider too, how often a
raw Performance has been extoll'd by the Partiality of private
Friendſhip; and what a Clamour of Injury has been rais'd
from that Quarter, upon ſuch Performance meeting a Repulſe;
we may pretty eaſily account for the Grounds upon which they
proceeded in diſcountenancing ſome Plays, and the harſh Things
that are thrown out upon their giving a Repulſe to others.

But I ſhould beg Pardon for interfering in this Queſtion, in
which I am properly neither Party nor Judge. I am only
throwing out a private Opinion, without Intereſt or Prejudice,
and if I am right in the Notion, *Valeat quantum valere poteſt.*

PRO.

PROLOGUE.

Written by *PHILIP FROWDE*, Efq;

And Spoken by Mr. WILKS.

A S in *some Region, where indulgent Skies*
  Enrich the Soil, a thousand Plants arise
Frequent and bold; a thousand Landskips meet
Our ravisht View, irregularly sweet :
We gaze, divided, now on These, now Those;
While All one beauteous Wilderness compose.
  Such SHAKESPEARE's *Genius was :* —— *Let* Bri-
  tons *boast*
The glorious Birth, and, eager, strive who most
Shall celebrate his Verse; for while we raise
Trophies of Fame to him, ourselves we praise :
Display the Talents of a British *Mind,*
Where All is great, free, open, unconfin'd.
Be it our Pride, to reach his daring Flight;
And relish Beauties, he alone could write.
  Most modern Authors, fearful to aspire,
With Imitation cramp their genial Fire ;
The well-schemed Plan keep strict before their Eyes,
Dwell on Proportions, trifling Decencies;
While noble Nature all neglected lies.
Nature, that claims Precedency of Place,
Perfection's Basis, and essential Grace!

             Nature

PROLOGUE.

Nature so intimately SHAKESPEARE *knew,*
From her first Springs his Sentiments he drew;
Most greatly wild they flow; and, when most wild, yet
   true.

While These, secure in what the Criticks teach,
Of servile Laws still dread the dangerous Breach;
His vast, unbounded, Soul disdain'd their Rule,
Above the Precepts of the Pedant School!

Oh! could the Bard, revisiting our Light,
Receive these Honours done his Shade To-night,
How would he bless the Scene this Age displays,
Transcending his Eliza's *golden Days!*
When great AUGUSTUS *fills the* British *Throne,*
And his lov'd Consort *makes the Muse her own.*

How would he joy, to see fair Merit's Claim
Thus answer'd in his own reviving Fame!
How cry with Pride ——— " Oblivion I forgive;
" This my last Child to latest Times shall live:
" Lost to the World, well for the Birth it stay'd;
" To this auspicious *Æra* well delay'd.

EPI-

EPILOGUE.

Written by a Friend.

Spoken by Mrs. *OLDFIELD.*

WELL, *Heaven defend us from these ancient Plays,*
  These Moral Bards of good Queen Bess's *Days!*
They write from Virtue's Laws, and think no further;
But draw a Rape as dreadful as a Murther.
You modern Wits, more deeply vers'd in Nature,
Can tip the wink, to tell us, you know better;
As who shou'd say——" 'Tis no such killing Matter ——
" *We've heard old Stories told, and yet ne'er wonder'd,*
" *Of many a Prude, that has endur'd a Hundred:*
" *And* Violante *grieves, or we're mistaken,*
" *Not, because ravisht; but because ——forsaken.——*
 Had this been written to the modern Stage,
Her Manners had been copy'd from the Age.
Then, tho' she had been once a little wrong,
She still had had the Grace to've held her Tongue;
And after all, with downcast Looks, been led
Like any Virgin to the Bridal Bed.
There, if the good Man question'd her Mis-doing,
She'd stop him short——" Pray, who made you so knowing!
" *What, doubt my Virtue!—— What's your base Intention!*
" *Sir, that's a Point above your Comprehension.——*
           Well,

EPILOGUE.

Well, Heav'n be prais'd, the Virtue of our Times
Secures us from our Gothick Grandsires Crimes.
Rapes, Magick, new Opinions, which before
Have fill'd our Chronicles, are now no more:
And this reforming Age may justly boast,
That dreadful Sin Polygamy is lost.
So far from multiplying Wives, 'tis known
Our Husbands find, they've Work enough with one.——
Then, as for Rapes, those dangerous days are past;
Our Dapper Sparks are seldom in such haste.

In SHAKESPEARE's *Age the English Youth inspir'd,*
Lov'd, as they fought, by him and Beauty fir'd.
'Tis yours to crown the Bard, whose Magick Strain
Cou'd charm the Heroes of that glorious Reign,
Which humbled to the Dust the Pride of Spain.

Dra-

Dramatis Perſonæ.

M E N.

Duke *Angelo*.	Mr. *Corey*.
Roderick, his Elder Son.	Mr. *Mills*.
Henriquez, his Younger Son.	Mr. *Wilks*.
Don Bernard, Father to *Leonora*.	Mr. *Harper*.
Camillo, Father to *Julio*.	Mr. *Griffin*.
Julio, in Love with *Leonora*.	Mr. *Booth*.
Citizen.	Mr. *Oates*.
Maſter of the Flocks.	Mr. *Bridgwater*
Firſt Shepherd.	Mr. *Norris*.
Second Shepherd.	Mr. *Ray*.

W O M E N.

Leonora.	Mrs. *Porter*.
Violante.	Mrs. *Booth*.

SCENE, *the Province of* Andaluſia *in* Spain.

DOUBLE

DOUBLE FALSHOOD;

OR,

The DISTREST LOVERS.

ACT I. SCENE I.

SCENE, *A Royal Palace.*

Duke Angelo, Roderick, *and Courtiers.*

RODERICK.

Y gracious Father, this unwonted Strain
Visits my Heart with Sadness.
    Duke. —— Why, my Son?
Making my Death familiar to my Tongue
Digs not my Grave one Jot before the Date.
I've worn the Garland of my Honours long,
And would not leave it wither'd to thy Brow,
But flourishing and green; worthy the Man,

B   Who,

Who, with my Dukedoms, heirs my better Glories.

Roder. This Praife, which is my Pride, fpreads me
    with Blufhes.

Duke. Think not, that I can flatter thee, my *Roderick*;
Or let the Scale of Love o'er-poize my Judgment.
Like a fair Glafs of Retrofpection, Thou
Reflect'ft the Virtues of my early Youth;
Making my old Blood mend its Pace with Tranfport:
While fond *Henriquez*, thy irregular Brother,
Sets the large Credit of his Name at Stake,
A Truant to my Wifhes, and his Birth.
His Taints of Wildnefs hurt our nicer Honour,
And call for fwift Reclaim.

Roder. ———————— I truft, my Brother
Will, by the Vantage of his cooler Wifdom,
E'er-while redeem the hot Efcapes of Youth,
And court Opinion with a golden Conduct.

Duke. Be Thou a Prophet in that kind Suggeftion!
But I, by Fears weighing his unweigh'd Courfe,
Interpret for the Future from the Paft.
And ftrange Mifgivings, why he hath of late
By Importunity, and ftrain'd Petition,
Wrefted our Leave of Abfence from the Court,
Awake Sufpicion. Thou art inward with him;
And, haply, from the bofom'd Truft can'ft fhape
Some formal Caufe to qualify my Doubts.

Roder. Why he hath prefs'd this Abfence, Sir, I
    know not;
But have his Letters of a modern Date,
Wherein by *Julio*, good *Camillo*'s Son,
(Who, as he fays, fhall follow hard upon;
And whom I with the growing Hour expect:)
He doth follicit the Return of Gold
To purchafe certain Horfe, that like him well.
This *Julio* he encounter'd firft in *France*,
And lovingly commends him to my Favour;
Wifhing I would detain him fome few Days,
To know the Value of his well-placed Truft.

Duke.

Duke. O, do it, *Roderick*; and affay to mould him
An honeft Spy upon thy Brother's Riots.
Make us acquainted when the Youth arrives;
We'll fee this *Julio*, and he fhall from Us
Receive the fecret Loan his Friend requires.
Bring him to Court.

                               [*Exeunt.*

SCENE II. *Profpect of a Village at a Diftance.*

Enters Camillo *with a Letter.*

Cam. How comes the Duke to take fuch Notice of
my Son, that he muft needs have him in Court, and I
muft fend him upon the View of his Letter? ——
Horfemanfhip! What Horfemanfhip has *Julio?* I think,
he can no more but gallop a Hackney, unlefs he practifed
Riding in *France.* It may be, he did fo; for he was
there a good Continuance. But I have not heard him
fpeak much of his Horfemanfhip. That's no Matter: if he be not a good Horfeman, all's one in fuch
a Cafe, he muft bear. Princes are abfolute; they
may do what they will in any Thing, fave what they
cannot do.

Enters Julio.

O, come on, Sir; read this Paper: no more Ado, but
read it: It muft not be anfwer'd by my Hand, nor
yours, but, in Grofs, by your Perfon; your fole Perfon. Read aloud.

Jul. 'Pleafe you, to let me firft o'erlook it, Sir.

Cam. I was this other day in a Spleen againft your
new Suits: I do now think, fome Fate was the Taylour
that hath fitted them: for, this Hour, they are for
the Palace of the Duke. —— Your Father's Houfe is
too dufty.

                                           Jul.

Jul. Hem!— to Court? Which is the better, to ferve a Miftrefs, or a Duke? I am fued to be his Slave, and I fue to be *Leonora's*.   [*Afide.*

Cam. You fhall find your Horfemanfhip much praifed there; Are you fo good a Horfeman?

Jul. I have been,
E'er now, commended for my Seat, or mock'd.

Cam. Take one Commendation with another, every Third's a Mock.— Affect not therefore to be praifed. Here's a deal of Command and Entreaty mixt; there's no denying; you muft go, peremptorily he inforces That

Jul. What Fortune foever my Going fhall encounter, cannot be good Fortune; What I part withal unfeafons any other Goodnefs.   [*Afide.*

Cam. You muft needs go; he rather conjures, than importunes.

Jul. No moving of my Love-Suit to him now?—
                                                                [*Afide.*

Cam. Great Fortunes have grown out of lefs Grounds.

Jul. What may her Father think of me, who expects to be follicited this very Night?   [*Afide.*

Cam. Thofe fcatter'd Pieces of Virtue, which are in him, the Court will folder together, varnifh, and rectify.

Jul. He will furely think I deal too flightly, or unmannerly, or foolifhly, indeed; nay, difhoneftly; to bear him in hand with my Father's Confent, who yet hath not been touch'd with fo much as a Requeft to it.   [*Afide.*

Cam. Well, Sir, have you read it over?

Jul. Yes, Sir.

Cam. And confider'd it?

Jul. As I can.

Cam. If you are courted by good Fortune, you muft go.

Jul. So it pleafe You, Sir.

                                                                Cam.

Cam. By any Means, and to morrow: Is it not there the Limit of his Requeſt?

Jul. It is, Sir.

Cam. I muſt bethink me of ſome Neceſſaries, without which you might be unfurniſh'd: And my Supplies ſhall at all Convenience follow You. Come to my Cloſet by and by; I would there ſpeak with You.
[*Exit* Camillo.

Manet Julio *ſolus.*

Jul. I do not ſee that Fervour in the Maid,
Which Youth and Love ſhould kindle. She conſents,
As 'twere to feed without an Appetite;
Tells me, She is content; and plays the Coy one,
Like Thoſe that ſubtly make their Words their Ward,
Keeping Addreſs at Diſtance. This Affection
Is ſuch a feign'd One, as will break untouch'd;
Dye froſty, e'er it can be thaw'd; while mine,
Like to a Clime beneath *Hyperion*'s Eye,
Burns with one conſtant Heat. I'll ſtrait go to her;
Pray her to regard my Honour: but She greets me.—

Enter Leonora, *and Maid.*

See, how her Beauty doth inrich the Place!
O, add the Muſick of thy charming Tongue,
Sweet as the Lark that wakens up the Morn,
And make me think it Paradiſe indeed.
I was about to ſeek thee, *Leonora,*
And chide thy Coldneſs, Love.

Leon. ————— What ſays your Father?

Jul. I have not mov'd him yet.

Leon. ————— Then do not, *Julio.*

Jul. Not move him? Was it not your own Command,
That his Conſent ſhould ratify our Loves?

Leon. Perhaps, it was: but now I've chang'd my Mind.
You purchaſe at too dear a Rate, that puts You
To wooe me and your Father too: Beſides,
As He, perchance, may ſay, you ſhall not have me;
B 3 You,

You, who are fo obedient, muft difcharge me
Out of your Fancy : Then, you know, 'twill prove
My Shame and Sorrow, meeting fuch Repulfe,
To wear the Willow in my Prime of Youth.

    Jul. Oh! do not rack me with thefe ill-placed
        Doubts;
Nor think, tho' Age has in my Father's Breaft
Put out Love's Flame, he therefore has not Eyes,
Or is in Judgment blind. You wrong your Beauties,
Venus will frown if you difprize her Gifts,
That have a Face would make a frozen Hermit
Leap from his Cell, and burn his Beads to kifs it;
Eyes, that are nothing but continual Births
Of new Defires in Thofe that view their Beams.
You cannot have a Caufe to doubt.

    Leon. —————————————Why, *Julio?*
When you that dare not chufe without your Father,
And, where you love, you dare not vouch it; muft not,
Though you have Eyes, fee with 'em; — can I, think
        you,
Somewhat, perhaps, infected with your Suit,
Sit down content to fay, You would, but dare not?

    Jul. Urge not Sufpicions of what cannot be;
You deal unkindly; mis-becomingly,
I'm loth to fay: For All that waits on you,
Is graced, and graces. —— No Impediment
Shall bar my Wifhes, but fuch grave Delays
As Reafon prefles Patience with; which blunt not,
But rather whet our Loves. Be patient, Sweet.

    Leon Patient! What elfe? My Flames are in the Flint.
Haply, to lofe a Husband I may weep;
Never, to get One: When I cry for Bondage,
Let Freedom quit me.

    Jul. ———————— From what a Spirit comes This?
I now perceive too plain, you care not for me.
Duke, I obey thy Summons, be its Tenour
Whate'er it will: If War, I come thy Souldier:
Or if to wafte my filken Hours at Court,

                       The

The Slave of Fashion, I with willing Soul
Embrace the lazy Banishment for Life;
Since *Leonora* has pronounc'd my Doom.

    Leon. What do you mean? Why talk you of the
      Duke?
Wherefore of War, or Court, or Banishment?

    Jul. How this new Note is grown of me, I know
      not;
But the Duke writes for Me.   Coming to move
My Father in our Bus'ness, I did find him
Reading this Letter; whose Contents require
My instant Service, and Repair to Court.

    Leon. Now I perceive the Birth of these Delays;
Why *Leonora* was not worth your Suit.
Repair to Court? Ay, there you shall, perhaps,
(Rather, past Doubt;) behold some choicer Beauty,
Rich in her Charms, train'd to the Arts of Soothing,
Shall prompt you to a Spirit of Hardiness,
To say, So please you, Father, I have chosen
This Mistress for my own. ——

    Jul. —— —————— Still you mistake me:
Ever your Servant I profess my self;
And will not blot me with a Change, for all
That Sea and Land inherit.

    Leon. But when go you?

    Jul. To morrow, Love; so runs the Duke's Com-
      mand;
Stinting our Farewell-kisses, cutting off
The Forms of Parting, and the Interchange
Of thousand precious Vows, with Haste too rude.
Lovers have Things of Moment to debate,
More than a Prince, or dreaming Statesman, know:
Such Ceremonies wait on *Cupid*'s Throne.
Why heav'd that Sigh?

    Leon. O *Julio*, let me whisper
What, but for Parting, I should blush to tell thee:
My Heart beats thick with Fears, left the gay Scene,
The Splendors of a Court, should from thy Breast

            Banish

Banifh my Image, kill my Int'reft in thee,
And I be left, the Scoff of Maids, to drop
A Widow's Tear for thy departed Faith.

Jul. O let Affurance, ftrong as Words can bind,
Tell thy pleas'd Soul, I will be wond'rous faithful;
True, as the Sun is to his Race of Light,
As Shade to Darknefs, as Defire to Beauty:
And when I fwerve, let Wretchednefs o'ertake me,
Great as e'er Falfhood met, or Change can merit.

Leon. Enough; I'm fatisfied: and will remain
Yours, with a firm and untir'd Conftancy.
Make not your Abfence long: Old Men are wav'ring;
And fway'd by Int'reft more than Promife giv'n.
Should fome frefh Offer ftart, when you're away,
I may be preft to Something, which muft put
My Faith, or my Obedience, to the Rack.

Jul. Fear not, but I with fwifteft Wing of Time
Will labour my Return. And in my Abfence,
My noble Friend, and now our honour'd Gueft,
The Lord *Henriquez*, will in my behalf
Hang at your Father's Ear, and with kind Hints,
Pour'd from a friendly Tongue, fecure my Claim;
And play the Lover for thy abfent *Julio*.

Leon. Is there no Inftance of a Friend turn'd falfe?
Take Heed of That : No Love by Proxy, *Julio.*
My Father——

Enters Don Bernard.

D. Bern. What, *Julio*, in publick? This Wooeing is
too urgent. Is your Father yet moved in the Suit,
who muft be the prime Unfolder of this Bufinefs?

Jul. I have not yet, indeed, at full poffefs'd
My Father, whom it is my Service follows;
But only that I have a Wife in Chafe.

D. Bern. Chafe! —— Let Chafe alone: No Matter for That.—— You may halt after her, whom
you profefs to purfue, and catch her too; Marry, not
unlefs

unlefs your Father let you flip.———— Briefly, I defire
you, (for fhe tells me, my Inftructions fhall be both
Eyes and Feet to her;) no farther to infift in your Re-
quiring, 'till, as I have formerly faid, *Camillo* make
known to Me, that his good Liking goes along with
Us; which but once breath'd, all is done; 'till when,
the Bufinefs has no Life, and cannot find a Begin-
ning.

Jul. Sir, I will know his Mind, e'er I tafte Sleep:
At Morn, you fhall be learn'd in his Defire.
I take my Leave.————O virtuous *Leonora*,
Repofe, fweet as thy Beauties, feal thy Eyes;
Once more, adieu. I have thy Promife, Love;
Remember, and be faithful.   [*Ex.* Julio.

D. Bern. His Father is as unfettled, as he is way-
ward, in his Difpofition. If I thought young *Julio*'s
Temper were not mended by the Mettal of his Mother, I fhould be fomething crazy in giving my Confent to this Match: And, to tell you true, if my Eyes
might be the Directors to your Mind, I could in this
Town look upon Twenty Men of more delicate Choice.
I fpeak not This altogether to unbend your Affections
to him: But the Meaning of what I fay is, that you
fet fuch Price upon yourfelf to him, as Many, and much
his Betters, would buy you at; (and reckon thofe Virtues in you at the rate of their Scarcity;) to which if
he come not up, you remain for a better Mart.

Leon. My Obedience, Sir, is chain'd to your Ad-
vice.

D. Bern. 'Tis well faid, and wifely. I fear, your
Lover is a little Folly-tainted; which, fhortly after it
proves fo, you will repent.

Leon. Sir, I confefs, I approve him of all the Men
I know; but that Approbation is nothing, 'till feafon'd
by your Confent.

D. Bern. We fhall hear foon what his Father will
do, and fo proceed accordingly. I have no great Heart
to the Bufinefs, neither will I with any Violence op-
pofe

pofe it : But leave it to that Power which rules in thefe
Conjunctions, and there's an End. Come; hafte We
homeward, Girl. 　　　　　　　　　　　*[Exeunt.*

SCENE III.

Enter Henriquez, *and Servants with Lights.*

Henr. Bear the Lights clofe : ——— Where is the
　　　Mufick, Sirs?
Serv. Coming, my Lord.
Henr. Let 'em not come too near. This Maid,
For whom my Sighs ride on the Night's chill Vapour,
Is born moft humbly, tho' fhe be as fair
As Nature's richeft Mould and Skill can make her,
Mended with ftrong Imagination.
But what of That? Th' Obfcurenefs of her Birth
Cannot eclipfe the Luftre of her Eyes,
Which make her all One Light. ——— Strike up, my
　　　Mafters;
But touch the Strings with a religious Softnefs;
Teach Sound to languifh thro' the Night's dull Ear,
'Till Melancholy ftart from her lazy Couch,
And Carelefsnefs grow Convert to Attention.
　　　　　　　　　　　[Mufick plays.
She drives me into Wonder, when I fometimes
Hear her difcourfe; The Court, whereof Report,
And Guefs alone inform her, fhe will rave at,
As if fhe there fev'n Reigns had flander'd Time.
Then, when fhe reafons on her Country State,
Health, Virtue, Plainnefs, and Simplicity,
On Beauties true in Title, fcorning Art,
Freedom as well to do, as think, what's good;
My Heart grows fick of Birth and empty Rank,
And I become a Villager in Wifh.
Play on; ——— She fleeps too found : —— Be ftill,
　　　and vanifh :

　　　　　　　　　　　　　　　　　A

A Gleam of Day breaks fudden from her Window:
O Taper, graced by that midnight Hand!

Violante *appears above at her Window.*

Viol. Who is't, that wooes at this late Hour? What
   are you?

Henr. One, who for your dear Sake ———

Viol. Watches the ftarlefs Night!
My Lord *Henriquez*, or my Ear deceives me.
You've had my Anfwer, and 'tis more than ftrange
You'll combat thefe Repulfes.   Good my Lord,
Be Friend to your own Health ; and give me Leave,
Securing my poor Fame, nothing to pity
What Pangs you fwear you fuffer. 'Tis impoffible
To plant your choice Affections in my Shade,
At leaft, for them to grow there.

Henr. ——————————— Why, *Violante?*

Viol. Alas! Sir, there are Reafons numberlefs
To bar your Aims. Be warn'd to Hours more wholefom ;
For, Thefe you watch in vain.   I have read Stories,
(I fear, too true ones;) how young Lords, like you,
Have thus befung mean Windows, rhymed their Suf-
   ferings
Ev'n to th'Abufe of Things Divine, fet up
Plain Girls, like me, the Idols of their Worfhip,
Then left them to bewail their eafie Faith,
And ftand the World's Contempt.

Henr. ——————————— Your Memory,
Too faithful to the Wrongs of few loft Maids,
Makes Fear too general.

Viol. ——————— Let us be homely,
And let us too be chaft, doing you Lords no Wrong;
But crediting your Oaths with fuch a Spirit,
As you profefs them: fo no Party trufted
Shall make a lofing Bargain. Home, my Lord,
What you can fay, is moft unfeafonable; what fing,
Moft abfonant and harfh : Nay, your Perfume,
Which I fmell hither, cheers not my Senfe
Like our Field-violet's Breath.

                                                  Henr.

Henr. ———— ———— ——Why, this Difmiffion
Does more invite my Staying.
Viol. ———— ———— ——Men of your Temper
Make ev'ry Thing their Bramble. But I wrong
That which I am preferving, my Maid's Name,
To hold fo long Difcourfe. Your Virtues guide you
T'effect fome nobler Purpofe! [*Ex.* Violante.
Henr. Stay, bright Maid!
Come back, and leave me with a fairer Hope.
She's gone: —— Who am I, that am thus contemn'd?
The fecond Son to a Prince? —— Yes; well; What
then?
Why, your great Birth forbids you to defcend
To a low Alliance: —— Her's is the felf-fame Stuff,
Whereof we Dukes are made; but Clay more pure!
And take away my Title, which is acquir'd
Not by my felf, but thrown by Fortune on Me,
Or by the Merit of fome Anceftour
Of fingular Quality, She doth inherit
Deferts t'outweigh me. —— I muft ftoop to gain her;
Throw all my gay Comparifons afide,
And turn my proud Additions out of Service,
Rather than keep them to become my Mafters.

The Dignities we wear, are Gifts of Pride;
And laugh'd at by the Wife, as meer Outfide.
[*Exit*

End of the Firft A&t.

ACT

ACT II. SCENE I.

SCENE, *The Prospect of a Village.*

Enter Fabian *and* Lopez; Henriquez *on the Opposite Side.*

Lop. SOFT, soft you, Neighbour; who comes
here? Pray you, slink aside.

Henr. Ha! Is it come to this? Oh the Devil, the
Devil, the Devil!

Fab. Lo you now! for Want of the discreet Ladle
of a cool Understanding, will this Fellow's Brains
boil over.

Henr. To have enjoy'd her, I would have given——
What?
All that at present I could boast my own,
And the Reversion of the World to boot,
Had the Inheritance been mine:—— And now,
(Just Doom of guilty Joys!) I grieve as much
That I have rifled all the Stores of Beauty,
Those Charms of Innocence and artless Love,
As just before I was devour'd with Sorrow,
That she refus'd my Vows, and shut the Door
Upon my ardent Longings.

Lop. Love! Love!——Downright Love! I see by
the Foolishness of it.

Henr. Now then to Recollection——Was't not so?
A Promise first of Marriage—— Not a Promise only,
for 'twas bound with Surety of a thousand Oaths;——
and those not light ones neither.—— Yet I remember
too, those Oaths could not prevail; th' unpractis'd
Maid trembled to meet my Love: By Force alone I
snatch'd

ſnatch'd th' imperfeᵭ Joy, which now torments my
Memory. Not Love, but brutal Violence prevail'd;
to which the Time, and Place, and Opportunity,
were Acceſſaries moſt diſhonourable. Shame, Shame
upon it!

Fab. What a Heap of Stuff's this——I fancy, this
Fellow's Head would make a good Pedlar's Pack, Neighbour.

Henr. Hold, let me be ſevere to my Self, but not
unjuſt.——Was it a Rape then? No. Her Shrieks,
her Exclamations then had drove me from her. True,
ſhe did not conſent; as true, ſhe did reſiſt; but ſtill
in Silence all.———'Twas but the Coyneſs of a mo-
deſt Bride, not the Reſentment of a raviſht Maid.
And is the Man yet born, who would not riſque the
Guilt, to meet the Joy?——The Guilt! that's true
——but then the Danger; the Tears, the Clamours of
the ruin'd Maid, purſuing me to Court. That, that,
I fear will (as it already does my Conſcience) ſome-
thing ſhatter my Honour. What's to be done? But
now I have no Choice. Fair *Leonora* reigns confeſt the
Tyrant Queen of my revolted Heart, and *Violante*
ſeems a ſhort Uſurper there. —— *Julio*'s already by my
Arts remov'd.——O Friendſhip, how wilt thou anſwer That? Oh, that a Man could reaſon down this
Feaver of the Blood, or ſooth with Words the Tumult in his Heart! Then, *Julio*, I might be, indeed,
thy Friend. They, they only ſhould condemn me, who
born devoid of Paſſion ne'er have prov'd the fierce
Diſputes 'twixt Virtue and Deſire. While they, who
have, like me,

The looſe Eſcapes of youthful Nature known.
Muſt wink at mine, indulgent to their own.

[*Exit* Henriquez.

Lop. This Man is certainly mad, and may be miſ-
chievous. Pr'ythee, Neighbour, let's follow him;
but at ſome Diſtance, for fear of the worſt.

[*Exeunt, after* Henr.

SCENE

S C E N E II.   *An Apartment.*

Enters Violante *alone.*

Viol. Whom fhall I look upon without a Blufh?
There's not a Maid, whofe Eye with Virgin Gaze
Pierces not to my Guilt. What will't avail me,
To fay I was not willing;
Nothing; but that I publifh my Difhonour,
And wound my Fame anew. ——O Mifery,
To feem to all one's Neighbours rich, yet know
One's Self neceffitous and wretched.

Enter Maid, and afterwards Gerald *with a Letter.*

Maid. Madam, here's *Gerald*, Lord *Henriquez'* Ser-
     vant;
He brings a Letter to you.
   Viol. A Letter to me! How I tremble now!
Your Lord's for Court, good *Gerald*, is he not?
   Ger. Not fo, Lady.
   Viol. O my prefaging Heart! When goes he then?
   Ger. His Bufinefs now fteers him fome other Courfe.
   Viol. Whither, I pray you? —How my Fears tor-
     ment me!
   Ger. Some two Months Progrefs.
   Viol. ——— ——————Whither, whither, Sir,
I do befeech you? Good Heav'ns, I lofe all Patience.
Did he deliberate this? or was the Bufinefs
But then conceiv'd, when it was born?
   Ger. Lady, I know not That; nor is it in the Com-
mand I have to wait your Anfwer. For the perufing
the Letter I commend you to your Leifure.
                                        [*Exit* Gerald.
   Viol. To Hearts like mine Sufpence is Mifery.
Wax, render up thy Truft: Be the Contents
Profp'rous, or fatal, they are all my Due.
                                        Reads.]

Reads.] *Our Prudence should now teach us to forget,*
what our Indiscretion has committed.   I
have already made one Step towards this
Wisdom, by prevailing on Myself to bid you
                                    Farewell.

O, Wretched and betray'd! Loft *Violante!*
Heart-wounded with a thousand perjur'd Vows,
Poison'd with studied Language, and bequeath'd
To Desperation.   I am now become
The Tomb of my own Honour: a dark Mansion,
For Death alone to dwell in.   I invite thee,
Consuming Desolation, to this Temple,
Now fit to be thy Spoil: the ruin'd Fabrick,
Which cannot be repair'd, at once o'er-throw.
What must I do? —— But That's not worth my
        Thought:
I will commend to Hazard all the Time
That I shall spend hereafter: Farewel, my Father,
Whom I'll no more offend: and Men, adieu,
Whom I'll no more believe: and Maids, adieu,
Whom I'll no longer shame.   The Way I go,
As yet I know not. —— Sorrow be my Guide.
                                [*Exit* Violante.

S C E N E III. *Prospect of a Village,* before
Don Bernard's *House.*

Enters Henriquez.

Henr. Where were the Eyes, the Voice, the va-
        rious Charms,
Each beauteous Particle, each namelefs Grace,
Parents of glowing Love? All Thefe in Her,
It feems, were not: but a Difeafe in Me,
That fancied Graces in her. —— Who ne'er beheld
More than a Hawthorne, fhall have Caufe to fay
The Cedar's a tall Tree; and fcorn the Shade,
                                        The

The lov'd Bufh once had lent him. Soft! mine Ho-
　nour
Begins to ficken in this black Reflection.
How can it be, that with my Honour fafe
I fhould purfue *Leonora* for my Wife ?
That were accumulating Injuries,
To *Violante* firft, and now to *Julio*;
To her a perjur'd Wretch, to him perfidious;
And to myfelf in ftrongeft Terms accus'd
Of murth'ring Honour wilfully, without which
My Dog's the Creature of the nobler Kind. ——
But Pleafure is too ftrong for Reafon's Curb ;
And　Confcience　finks　o'er-power'd　with　Beauty's
　Sweets.
Come, *Leonora*, Authrefs of my Crime,
Appear, and vindicate thy Empire here;
Aid me to drive this ling'ring Honour hence,
And I am wholly thine.

　　　Enter to him, Don Bernard *and* Leonora.

　　D. Bern. Fye, my good Lord; why would you wait
　　　without?
If you fufpect your Welcome, I have brought
My *Leonora* to affure you of it.　　[Henr. *falutes* Leon.
　　Henr. O Kifs, fweet as the Odours of the Spring,
But cold as Dews that dwell on Morning Flow'rs!
Say, *Leonora*, has your Father conquer'd?
Shall Duty then at laft obtain the Prize,
Which you refus'd to Love? And fhall *Henriquez*
Owe all his Happinefs to good *Bernardo* ?
Ah! no; I read my Ruin in your Eyes:
That Sorrow, louder than a thoufand Tongues,
Pronounces my Defpair.
　　D. Bern. ——————Come, *Leonora*,
You are not now to learn, this noble Lord,
(Whom but to name, reftores my failing Age,)
Has with a Lover's Eye beheld your Beauty;
　　　　　　　　　C　　　　　　　　　Thro

Thro' which his Heart fpeaks more than Language
    can ;
It offers Joy and Happinefs to You,
And Honour to our Houfe.   Imagine then
The Birth and Qualities of him that loves you;
Which when you know, you cannot rate too dear.

    Leon. My Father, on my Knees I do befeech you
To paufe one Moment on your Daughter's Ruin.
I vow, my Heart ev'n bleeds, that I muft thank you
For your paft Tendernefs; and yet diftruft
That which is yet behind.   Confider, Sir,
Whoe'er's th' Occafion of another's Fault,
Cannot himfelf be innocent.   O, give not
The cenfuring World Occafion to reproach
Your harfh Commands; or to my Charge lay That
Which moft I fear, the Fault of Difobedience.

    D. Bern. Pr'ythee, fear neither the One, nor the O-
ther: I tell thee, Girl, there's more Fear than Danger.   For my own part, as foon as Thou art married
to this noble Lord, my Fears will be over.

    Leon. Sir, I fhould be the vaineft of my Sex,
Not to efteem myfelf unworthy far
Of this high Honour.   Once there was a Time,
When to have heard my Lord *Henriquez'* Vows,
Might have fubdued my unexperienc'd Heart,
And made me wholly his. —— But That's now paft:
And my firm-plighted Faith by your Confent
Was long fince given to the injur'd *Julio.*

    D. Bern. Why then, by my Confent e'en take it
back again. Thou, like a fimple Wench, haft given thy
Affections to a Fellow, that does not care a Farthing
for them.   One, that has left thee for a Jaunt to
Court; as who fhould fay, I'll get a Place now ; 'tis
Time enough to marry, when I'm turn'd out of it.

    Henr. So, furely, it fhould feem, moft lovely Maid;
Julio, alas, feels nothing of my Paffion:
His Love is but th' Amufement of an Hour,
A fhort Relief from Bufinefs, or Ambition,

The

The Sport of Youth, and Fashion of the Age.
O! had he known the Hopes, the Doubts, the Ar-
   dours,
Or half the fond Varieties of Passion,
That play the Tyrant with my tortur'd Soul;
He had not left Thee to pursue his Fortune:
To practise Cringes in a slavish Circle,
And barter real Bliss for unsure Honour.
   Leon. Oh, the opposing Wind,
Should'ring the Tide, makes here a fearful Billow:
I needs must perish in it.——Oh, my Lord,
Is it then possible, you can forget
What's due to your great Name, and princely Birth,
To Friendship's holy Law, to Faith repos'd,
To Truth, to Honour, and poor injur'd *Julio?*
O think, my Lord, how much this *Julio* loves you;
Recall his Services, his well-try'd Faith;
Think too, this very Hour, where-e'er he be,
Your Favour is the Envy of the Court,
And secret Triumph of his grateful Heart.
Poor *Julio*, how securely thou depend'st
Upon the Faith and Honour of thy Master;
Mistaken Youth! this very Hour he robs thee
Of all thy Heart holds dear.— 'Tis so *Henriquez*
Repays the Merits of unhappy *Julio*.   [*Weeps.*
   Henr. My slumb'ring Honour catches the Alarm.
I was to blame to parley with her thus:
Sh'as shown me to myself. It troubles me.   [*Aside.*
   D. Bern. Mad; Mad. Stark mad, by this Light.
   Leon. I but begin to be so. — I conjure you,
By all the tender Interests of Nature,
By the chaste Love 'twixt you, and my dear Mother,
(O holy Heav'n, that she were living now!)
Forgive and pity me.—— Oh, Sir, remember,
I've heard my Mother say a thousand Times,
Her Father would have forced her Virgin Choice;
But when the Conflict was 'twixt Love and Duty,
Which should be first obey'd, my Mother quickly

Paid up her Vows to Love, and married You.
You thought this well, and she was praised for This;
For this her Name was honour'd, Disobedience
Was ne'er imputed to her, her firm Love
Conquer'd whate'er oppos'd it, and she prosper'd
Long Time your Wife. My Case is now the same;
You are the Father, which You then condemn'd;
I, what my Mother was; but not so happy.——

D. Bern. Go to, you're a Fool. No doubt, You
have old Stories enough to undo you. —— What, you
can't throw yourself away but by Precedent, ha?—
You will needs be married-to One, that will None of
You? You will be happy no Body's way but your
own, forsooth.—— But, d'ye mark me, spare your
Tongue for the future; (and That's using you hardly
too, to bid you spare what you have a great deal too
much of:) Go, go your ways, and d'ye hear, get
ready within these Two days to be married to a Husband you don't deserve;—Do it, or, by my dead Father's Soul, you are no Acquaintance of mine.

Henr. She weeps: Be gentler to her, good *Bernardo.*

Leon. Then Woe the Day.—— I'm circled round
    with Fire;
No Way for my Escape, but thro' the Flames.
Oh, can I e'er resolve to live without
A Father's Blessing, or abandon *Julio?*
With other Maids, the Choice were not so hard;
Int'rest, that rules the World, has made at last
A Merchandize of Hearts: and Virgins now
Chuse as they're bid, and wed without Esteem.
By nobler Springs shall my Affections move;
Nor own a Master, but the Man I love.
                      [Exit Leonora.

D. Bern. Go thy ways, Contradiction. —— Follow
her, my Lord; follow her, in the very Heat. This
Obstinacy must be combated by Importunity as obsti-
nate.   *[Exit* Henriquez *after her.*
                            The

The Girl fays right; her Mother was juft fuch A-
nother. I remember, Two of Us courted her at the
fame Time. She lov'd neither of Us, but She chofe
me purely to fpight that furly Old Blockhead my Fa-
ther-in-Law. Who comes here, *Camillo?* Now the
refufing Part will lie on my Side.——

Enters Camillo.

Cam. My worthy Neighbour, I am much in Fortune's Favour to find You thus alone. I have a Suit
to You.

D. Bern. Pleafe to name it, Sir.

Cam. Sir, I have long held You in fingular Efteem:
and what I fhall now fay, will be a Proof of it. You
know, Sir, I have but one Son.

D. Bern. Ay, Sir.

Cam. And the Fortune I am bleft withal, You pretty well know what it is.

D. Bern. 'Tis a fair One, Sir.

Cam. Such as it is, the whole Reverfion is my Son's.
He is now engaged in his Attendance on our Mafter,
the Duke. But e'er he went, he left with me the
Secret of his Heart, his Love for your fair Daughter.
For your Confent, he faid, 'twas ready: I took a
Night, indeed, to think upon it, and now have brought
you mine; and am come to bind the Contract with
half my Fortune in prefent, the Whole fome time
hence, and, in the mean while, my hearty Bleffing.
Ha? What fay You to't, *Don Bernard?*

D. Bern. Why, really, Neighbour,— I muft own, I
have heard Something of this Matter.——

Cam. Heard Something of it? No doubt, you have.

D. Bern. Yes, now I recollect it well.

Cam. Was it fo long ago then?

D. Bern. Very long ago, Neighbour.—— On *Tuef-
day* laft,

C 3   *Cam.*

Cam. What, am I mock'd in this Bufinefs, *Don Bernard* ?

D. Bern. Not mock'd, good *Camillo*, not mock'd: But in Love-matters, you know, there are Abundance of Changes in half an Hour. Time, Time, Neighbour, plays Tricks with all of us.

Cam. Time, Sir! What tell you me of Time? Come, I fee how this goes. Can a little Time take a Man by the Shoulder, and fhake off his Honour? Let me tell you, Neighbour, it muft either be a ftrong Wind, or a very mellow Honefty that drops fo eafily. Time, quoth'a?

D. Bern. Look'ee, *Camillo*; will you pleafe to put your Indignation in your Pocket for half a Moment, while I tell you the whole Truth of the Matter. My Daughter, you muft know, is fuch a tender Soul, fhe cannot poffibly fee a Duke's younger Son without falling defperately in Love with him. Now, you know, Neighbour, when Greatnefs rides Poft after a Man of my Years, 'tis both Prudence, and good Breeding, to let one's felf be overtaken by it. And who can help all This? I profefs, it was not my feeking, Neighbour.

Cam. I profefs, a Fox might earth in the Hollownefs of your Heart, Neighbour, and there's an End. If I were to give a bad Confcience its true Likenefs, it fhould be drawn after a very near Neighbour to a certain poor Neighbour of yours. —— Neighbour! with a Pox.

D. Bern. Nay, you are fo nimble with me, you will hear Nothing.

Cam. Sir, if I muft fpeak Nothing, I will hear Nothing. As for what you have to fay, if it comes from your Heart, 'tis a Lye before you fpeak it. — I'll to *Leonora*; and if I find her in the fame Story, why, I fhall believe your Wife was true to You, and your Daughter is your own. Fare you well. [*Exit, as into* D. Bernard's *Houfe.*

D. Bern.

D. Bern. Ay, but two Words muſt go to that Bargain. It happens, that I am at preſent of Opinion my Daughter ſhall receive no more Company to day at leaſt, no ſuch Viſits as yours.

[*Exit* D. Bernard, *following him*

SCENE IV. *Changes to another ProſpeEt of* Don Bernard's *Houſe.*

Leonora, *above.*

Leon. How tediouſly I've waited at the Window,
Yet know not One that paſſes.—— Should I truſt
My Letter to a Stranger, whom I think
To bear an honeſt Face, (in which ſometimes
We fancy we are wond'rous ſkilful;) then
I might be much deceiv'd. This late Example
Of baſe *Henriquez,* bleeding in me now,
From each good Aſpect takes away my Truſt:
For his Face ſeem'd to promiſe Truth and Honour.
Since Nature's Gifts in nobleſt Forms deceive,
Be happy You, that want 'em! —— Here comes One;
I've ſeen him, tho' I know him not; He has
An honeſt Face too—that's no Matter.—— Sir, ——

Enters Citizen.

Citiz. To me?
Leon. As You were of a virtuous Matron born,
(There is no Doubt, you are:) I do conjure you
Grant me one Boon. Say, do you know me, Sir?
Citiz. Ay, *Leonora,* and your worthy Father.
Leon. I have not Time to preſs the Suit I've to you
With many Words; nay, I ſhould want the Words,
Tho' I had Leiſure: but for Love of Juſtice,
And as you pity Miſery——But I wander
Wide from my Subject. Know you *Julio,* Sir?

Citiz.

Citiz. Yes, very well ; and love him too, as well.

Leon. Oh, there an Angel ſpake ! Then I conjure you,
Convey this Paper to him : and believe me,
You do Heav'n Service in't, and ſhall have Cauſe
Not to repent your Pains. —— I know not what
Your Fortune is ; —— Pardon me, gentle Sir,
That I am bold to offer This.

                       [*Throws down a Purſe with Money.*

D. Bern. within.] *Leonora.* ——

Leon. I truſt to you ; Heav'n put it in your Heart
To work me ſome Relief.

Citiz. Doubt it not, Lady. You have mov'd me ſo,
That tho' a thouſand Dangers barr'd my way,
I'd dare 'em all to ſerve you.   [*Exit Citizen.*

Leon. Thanks from a richer Hand than mine requite you !

D. Bern. within.] Why, Daughter ——

Leon. I come : — Oh, *Juiio*, feel but half my Grief,
And Thou wilt outfly Time to bring Relief.

                 [*Exit* Leonora *from the Window.*

End of the Second Act.

ACT

ACT III. SCENE I.

SCENE, *The Prospect of a Village.*

Enter Julio *with a Letter, and Citizen.*

Citiz. WHEN from the Window she did bow
and call,
Her Passions shook her Voice; and from her Eyes
Mistemper and Distraction, with strange Wildness
Bespoke Concern above a common Sorrow.

Jul. Poor *Leonora*! Treacherous, damn'd *Henriquez!*
She bids me fill my Memory with her Danger;
I do, my *Leonora*; yes, I fill
The Region of my Thought with nothing else;
Lower, she tells me here, that this Affair
Shall yield a Testimony of her Love:
And prays, her Letter may come safe and sudden.
This Pray'r the Heav'ns have heard, and I beseech 'em,
To hear all Pray'rs she makes.

Citiz. ——————————— Have Patience, Sir.

Jul. O my good Friend, methinks, I am too patient.
Is there a Treachery, like This in Baseness,
Recorded any where? It is the deepest:
None but Itself can be its Parallel:
And from a Friend, profess'd! ———— Friendship?
Why, 'tis
A Word for ever maim'd; in human Nature
It was a Thing the noblest; and 'mong Beasts,
It stood not in mean Place: Things of fierce Nature
Hold

Hold Amity and Concordance. —— Such a Villany
A Writer could not put down in his Scene,
Without Taxation of his Auditory
For Fiction moſt enormous.
    Citiz. ————————Theſe Upbraidings
Cool Time, while they are vented.
    Jul. ——————————I am counſel'd.
For you, evermore, Thanks. You've done much for Us;
So gently preſs'd to 't, that I may perſwade me
You'll do a little more.
    Cıtız. ———— Put me t'Employment
That's honeſt, tho' not ſafe, with my beſt Spirits
I'll give 't Accompliſhment.
    Jul. No more but This;
For I muſt ſee *Leonora*: And to appear
Like *Julio,* as I am, might haply ſpoil
Some good Event enſuing. Let me crave
Th' Exchange of Habit with you: ſome Diſguiſe,
May bear Me to my Love, unmark'd, and ſecret.
    Citiz. You ſhall not want. Yonder's the Houſe be-
      fore us:
Make Haſte to reach it.
    Jul. —————Still I thank you, Sir.
O *Leonora!* ſtand but this rude Shock;
Hold out thy Faith againſt the dread Aſſault
Of this baſe Lord, the Service of my Life
Shall be devoted to repay thy Conſtancy.   [*Exeunt.*

S C E N E II.   Don Bernard's *Houſe.*
Enters Leonora.

    Leon. I've hoped to th' lateſt Minute Hope can give:
He will not come: H'as not receiv'd my Letter:
May be, ſome other View has from our Home
Repeal'd his chang'd Eye: for what Buſineſs can
Excuſe a 'Tardineſs thus willfull? None.
Well then, it is not Buſineſs. —— Oh! that Let-
    ter, ————
I ſay, is not deliver'd; or He's ſick;

Or,

Or, O Suggeſtion, wherefore wilt Thou fright me?
Julio does to *Henriquez* on meer Purpoſe,
On plotted Purpoſe, yield me up; and He
Hath choſe another Miſtreſs.   All Preſumptions
Make pow'rful to this Point: His own Protraction,
Henriquez left behind; —— That Strain lack'd Jea-
    louſie,
Therefore lack'd Love. —— So ſure as Life ſhall
    empty
It ſelf in Death, this new Surmiſe of mine
Is a bold Certainty. 'Tis plain, and obvious,
Henriquez would not, durſt not, thus infringe
The Law of Friendſhip; thus provoke a Man,
That bears a Sword, and wears his Flag of Youth
As freſh as He: He durſt not: 'Tis Contrivance,
Groſs-dawbing 'twixt them Both.——But I'm o'er-
    heard.   [*Going.*

      Enters Julio, *diſguiſed.*

  Jul. Stay, *Leonora*; Has this outward Veil
Quite loſt me to thy Knowledge?
  Leon. ———————— O my *Julio!*
Thy Preſence ends the ſtern Debate of Doubt,
And cures me of a thouſand heartſick Fears,
Sprung from thy Abſence: yet awakes a Train
Of other ſleeping Terrors.   Do you weep?
  Jul. No, *Leonora*; when I weep, it muſt be
The Subſtance of mine Eye. 'Would I could weep;
For then mine Eye would drop upon my Heart,
And ſwage the Fire there.
  Leon. ————— You are full poſſeſs'd
How things go here. Firſt, welcome heartily;
Welcome to th'Ending of my laſt good Hour:
Now Summer Bliſs and gawdy Days are gone,
My Leaſe in 'em 's expir'd.
  Jul. ————— Not ſo, *Leonora.*
  Leon. Yes, *Julio*, yes; an everlaſting Storm
Is come upon me, which I can't bear out.
I cannot ſtay much Talk; we have loſt Leiſure;

                        And

And thus it is: Your Abſence hath giv'n Breeding
To what my Letter hath declar'd, and is
This Inſtant on th effecting, Hark! the Muſick
[*Flouriſh within.*
Is now on tuning, which muſt celebrate
This Buſ'neſs ſo diſcordant. ———Tell me then,
What you will do.
 Jul. ————— I know not what: Adviſe me:
I'll kill the Traytor.
 Leon. ————— O! take Heed: his Death
Betters our Cauſe no whit. No killing, *Julio.*
 Jul. My Blood ſtands ſtill; and all my Faculties
Are by Enchantment dull'd. You gracious Pow'rs,
The Guardians of ſworn Faith, and ſuff'ring Virtue,
Inſpire Prevention of this dreaded Miſchief!
This Moment is our own; Let's uſe it, Love,
And fly o'th' Inſtant from this Houſe of Woe.
 Leon. Alas! Impoſſible: My Steps are watch'd;
There's no Eſcape for Me. You muſt ſtay too.
 Jul. What! ſtay, and ſee thee raviſh'd from my Arms?
I'll force thy Paſſage. Wear I not a Sword?
Ne'er on Man's Thigh rode better. ——— If I ſuffer
The Traytor play his Part; if I not do
Manhood and Juſtice, Honour; let me be deem'd
A tame, pale, Coward, whom the Night-Owl's Hoot
May turn to Aſpen-leaf: Some Man take This,
Give Me a Diſtaff for it.
 Leon. ——— Patience, *Julio*;
And truſt to Me: I have fore-thought the Means
To diſappoint theſe Nuptials.———Hark! again;
[*Muſick within.*
Theſe are the Bells knoll for Us.———See, the Lights
Move this Way, *Julio.* Quick, behind yon Arras,
And take thy ſecret Stand. ———Diſpute it not;
I have my Reaſons, you anon ſhall know them: ——
There you may mark the Paſſages of the Night.
Yet, more: —— I charge you by the deareſt Tyes,
What-e'er you ſee, or hear, what-e'er ſhall hap,

In

In your Concealment reft a filent Statue.
Nay, hide thee ftrait, —or, —fee, I'm arm'd, and
    vow   [*Shews a Dagger.*
To fall a bleeding Sacrifice. before Thee.
               [*Thrufts him out, to the Arras.*
I dare not tell thee of my Purpofe, *Julio*,
Left it fhould wrap thee in fuch Agonies,
Which my Love could not look on. ———

SCENE *opens to a large Hall: An Altar pre-*
pared with Tapers. Enter at one Door Ser-
vants with Lights, Henriquez, Don Bernard,
and Churchman. At another, Attendants to
Leonora. Henriquez *runs to her.*

   Henr. Why, *Leonora,* wilt Thou with this Gloom
Darken my Triumph ; fuff'ring Difcontent,
And wan Difpleafure, to fubdue that Cheek
Where Love fhould fit inthron'd? Behold your Slave;
Nay, frown not; for each Hour of growing Time
Shall task me to thy Service, 'till by Merit
Of deareft Love I blot the low-born *Julio*
From thy fair Mind.
   Leon. ————So I fhall make it foul;
This Counfel is corrupt.
   Henr. —————Come, you will change.——
   Leon. Why would you make a Wife of fuch a One,
That is fo apt to change? This foul Proceeding
Still fpeaks againft itfelf, and vilifies
The pureft of your Judgment. —— For your Birth's
    Sake
I will not dart my hoarded Curfes at you,
Nor give my Meanings Language: For the Love
Of all good Things together, yet take heed,
And fpurn the Tempter back.
   D. Bern. I think, you're mad. —— Perverfe, and
    foolifh, Wretch !
                         Leon.

Leon. How may I be obedient, and wife too ?
Of my Obedience, Sir, I cannot ftrip me;
Nor can I then be wife: Grace againft Grace!
Ungracious, if I not obey a Father;
Moft perjur'd, if I do. ———— Yet, Lord, confider,
Or e'er too late, or e'er that Knot be ty'd,
Which may with Violence damnable be broken,
No other way diffever'd: Yet confider,
You wed my Body, not my Heart, my Lord;
No Part of my Affection.   Sounds it well,
That *Julio*'s Love is Lord *Henriquez*' Wife;
Have you an Ear for this harfh Sound?

Henr. No Shot of Reafon can come near the Place,
Where my Love's fortified.   The Day fhall come,
Wherein you'll chide this Backwardnefs, and blefs
Our Fervour in this Courfe.

Leon. ————————— No, no, *Henriquez*,
When you fhall find what Prophet you are prov'd,
You'll prophefie no more.

D. Bern. ——————Have done this Talking,
If you will cleave to your Obedience, do't;
If not, unbolt the Portal, and be gone;
My Blefling ftay behind you.

Leon. ————————— Sir, your Pardon:
I will not fwerve a Hair's Breadth from my Duty;
It fhall firft coft me dear.

D. Bern. ———————— Well then, to th' Point:
Give me your Hand. ——— My honour'd Lord, re-
ceive
My Daughter of Me, —— (nay, no dragging back,
But with my Curfes;) ——— whom I frankly give you,
And with you Joy and Honour.

  [*As* Don Bernard *goes to give* Leonora *to* Henriquez,
    Julio *advances from the Arras, and fteps between.*
Jul. ——————————Hold, *Don Bernard*,
Mine is the elder Claim.

D. Bern. ——————— What are you, Sir?

Jul.

Jul. A Wretch, that's almoſt loſt to his own Know-
ledge,
Struck thro' with Injuries. ———
    Henr. ——————— Ha! *Julio?* ——— Hear you,
Were you not ſent on our Commands to Court?
Order'd to wait your fair Diſmiſſion thence?
And have you dared, knowing you are our Vaſſal,
To ſteal away unpriviledg'd, and leave
My Buſineſs and your Duty unaccompliſh'd?
    Jul. Ungen'rous Lord! The Circumſtance of Things
Should ſtop the Tongue of Queſtion. ——— You have
wrong'd me;
Wrong'd me ſo baſely, in ſo dear a Point,
As ſtains the Cheek of Honour with a Bluſh;
Cancells the Bonds of Service; bids Allegiance
Throw to the Wind all high Reſpects of Birth,
Title, and Eminence; and, in their Stead,
Fills up the panting Heart with juſt Defiance.
If you have Senſe of Shame, or Juſtice, Lord,
Forego this bad Intent; or with your Sword
Anſwer me like a Man, and I ſhall thank you.
Julio once dead, *Leonora* may be thine;
But, living, She's a Prize too rich to part with.
    Henr. Vain Man! the preſent Hour is fraught with
Buſineſs
Of richer Moment. Love ſhall firſt be ſerv'd:
Then, if your Courage hold to claim it of me,
may have Leiſure to chaſtiſe this Boldneſs.
    Jul Nay, then I'll ſeize my Right.
    Henr. ——————— What, here, a Brawl?
My Servants, ——— Turn this boiſt'rous Sworder forth;
And ſee he come not to diſturb our Joys.
    Jul. Hold, Dogs! ——— *Leonora,* ——— Coward, baſe,
Henriquez!
        [Julio *is ſeiz'd, and drag'd out by the Servants.*
    Henr. She dies upon Me; help!
        [Leonora *ſwoons; as they endeavour to recover her,*
    a Paper drops from her.
                           D. Bern.

D. Bern. ———— Throng not about her;
But give her Air.
  Henr. ——What Paper's That? let's fee it.
It is her own Hand-Writing.
  D. Bern. ————————— Bow her Head:
'Tis but her Fright; fhe will recover foon.
What learn you by that Paper, good my Lord?
  Henr. That fhe would do the Violence to herfelf,
Which Nature hath anticipated on her.
What Dagger means fhe? Search her well, I pray
  you.
  D. Bern. Here is the Dagger. ———— Oh, the ftub-
  born Sex,
Rafh ev'n to Madnefs! ——
  Henr. ————————— Bear her to her Chamber:
Life flows in her again. ———— Pray, bear her hence:
And tend her, as you would the World's beft Treafure.
                    [*Women carry* Leonora *off.*
Don Bernard, this wild Tumult foon will ceafe,
The Caufe remov'd; and all return to Calmnefs.
Paffions in Women are as fhort in Working,
As ftrong in their Effect. Let the Prieft wait:
Come, go we in: My Soul is all on Fire;
And burns impatient of this forc'd Delay.
                    [*Exeunt; and the Scene clofes.*

S C E N E III. *Profpect of a Village at
a Diftance.*

Enters Roderick.

  Rod. *Julio's* Departure thus in fecret from Me,
With the long doubtful Abfence of my Brother,
(Who cannot fuffer, but my Father feels it;)
Have trufted me with ftrong Sufpicions,
And Dreams, that will not let me fleep, nor eat,
Nor tafte thofe Recreations Health demands:
                                        But,

But, like a Whirlwind, hither have they fnatch'd me,
Perforce, to be refolv'd. I know my Brother
Had *Julio*'s Father for his Hoft: from him
Enquiry may befriend me.

Enters Camillo.

Old Sir, I'm glad
To 've met you thus : What ails the Man? *Camillo*, ——
Cam. Ha?
Rod. Is't poffible, you fhould forget your Friends?
Cam. Friends! What are Thofe?
Rod. ———— Why, Thofe that love you, Sir.
Cam. You're None of Thofe, fure, if you be Lord
Roderick.
Rod. Yes, I am that Lord *Roderick*, and I lie not,
If I proteft, I love you paffing well.
Cam. You lov'd my Son too paffing well, I take it:
One, that believ'd too fuddenly his Court-Creed.
Rod. All is not well. [*afide.*] —— Good old Man,
do not rail.
Cam. My Lord, my Lord, you've dealt difho-
nourably.
Rod. Good Sir, I am fo far from doing Wrongs
Of that bafe Strain, I underftand you not.
Cam. Indeed! ———— You know not neither, o' my
Confcience,
How your moft virtuous Brother, noble *Henriquez*,
(You look fo like him, Lord, you are the worfe for't;
Rots upon fuch Diffemblers!) under colour
Of buying Courfers, and I know not what,
Bought my poor Boy out of Poffeffion
Ev'n of his plighted Faith. ———— Was not this Ho-
nour ?
And This a conftant Friend?
Rod ————————— I dare not fay fo.
Cam. Now you have robb'd him of his Love,
take all ;

Make

Make up your Malice, and difpatch his Life too.

Rod. If you would hear me, Sir,——

Cam. —— Your brave old Father
Would have been torn in Pieces with wild Horfes,
E'er he had done this Treachery. On my Confcience,
Had he but dreamt you Two durft have committed
This bafe, unmanly Crime, ——

Rod. Why, this is Madnefs. ——

Cam. I've done; I've eas'd my Heart; now you may
talk.

Rod. Then as I am a Gentleman, believe me,
(For I will lie for no Man;) I'm fo far
From being guilty of the leaft Sufpicion
Of Sin that way, that fearing the long Abfence
Of *Julio* and my Brother might beget
Something to ftart at, hither have I travell'd
To know the Truth of you.

Enters Violante *behind.*

Viol. My Servant loiters; fure, he means me well.
Camillo, and a Stranger? Thefe may give me
Some Comfort from their Talk. I'll ftep afide:
And hear what Fame is ftirring. [*Violante retires.*

Rod. —— Why this Wond'ring?

Cam. Can there be one fo near in Blood as you are
To that *Henriquez,* and an honeft Man?

Rod. While he was good, I do confefs my Near-
nefs;
But, fince his Fall from Honour, he's to me
As a ftrange Face I faw but Yefterday,
And as foon loft.

Cam. —— I ask your Pardon, Lord;
I was too rafh and bold.

Rod. —— —— No Harm done, Sir.

Cam. But is it poffible, you fhould not hear
The Paffage 'twixt *Leonora* and your Brother?

Rod. None of All This.

Enters

Enters Citizen.

Cam. How now?
Citiz. I bear you Tidings, Sir, which I could wish
Some other Tongue deliver'd.
    Cam. ———— Whence, I pray you?
Citiz. From your Son, Sir.
Cam. Pr'ythee, where is he?
Citiz. That's more than I know now, Sir.
But This I can assure you, he has left
The City raging mad; Heav'n comfort him!
He came to that curst Marriage——— The Fiends
    take it!———
    Cam. Pr'ythee, be gone, and bid the Bell knoll
    for me:
I have had one Foot in the Grave some Time.
Nay, go, good Friend; thy News deserve no Thanks.
How does your Lordship?   [*Exit Citizen.*
    Rod. ——— That's well said, Old Man.
I hope, all shall be well yet.
    Cam. ——— ——— ——— It had reed;
For 'tis a crooked World. Farewell, poor Boy!———

Enters Don Bernard.

    D. Bern. This comes of forcing Women where they
    hate:
It was my own Sin; and I am rewarded.
Now I am like an aged Oak, alone,
Left for all Tempests —— I would cry, but cannot:
I'm dry'd to Death almost with these Vexations.
Lord! what a heavy Load I have within me!
My Heart, — my Heart, — my Heart —
    Cam. ———Has this ill Weather
Met with Thee too?
    D. Bern. —— O Wench, that I were with thee!
    Cam. You do not come to mock at me now?
        D 2   *D. Bern.*

D. Bern. Ha?——

Cam. Do not diffemble; Thou may'ft find a Knave
As bad as thou art, to undo thee too:
I hope to fee that Day before I dye yet.

D. Bern. It needeth not, *Camillo*; I am Knave
Sufficient to my felf. If thou wilt rail,
Do it as bitterly as thou canft think of;
For I deferve it. Draw thy Sword, and ftrike me;
And I will thank thee for't. — I've loft my Daughter;
She's ftol'n away; and whither gone, I know not.

Cam. She has a fair Bleffing in being from you,
Sir.
I was too poor a Brother for your Greatnefs;
You muft be grafted into noble Stocks,
And have your Titles rais'd. My State was laugh'd at:
And my Alliance fcorn'd. I've loft a Son too;
Which muft not be put up fo. [*Offers to draw.*

Rod. —— Hold; be counfel'd.
You've equal Loffes; urge no farther Anger.
Heav'n, pleas'd now at your Love, may bring again,
And, no Doubt, will, your Children to your Com-
forts:
In which Adventure my Foot fhall be foremoft.
And One more will I add, my Honour'd Father;
Who has a Son to grieve for too, tho' tainted.
Let your joint Sorrow be as Balm to heal
Thefe Wounds of adverfe Fortune.

D. Bern. Come, *Camillo*,
Do not deny your Love, for Charity;
I ask it of you. Let this noble Lord
Make Brothers of Us, whom our own crofs Fates
Could never join. What I have been, forget;
What I intend to be, believe and nourifh:
I do confefs my Wrongs; give me your Hand.

Cam. Heav'n make thee honeft; —— there.

Rod. —— 'Tis done like good Men.
Now there refts Nought, but that we part, and each
Take

Take fev'ral Ways in Queft of our loft Friends:
Some of my Train o'er the wild Rocks fhall wait
    you.
Our beft Search ended, here we'll meet again,
And tell the Fortunes of our feparate Travels. [*Exeunt.*

Violante *comes forward.*

Viol. I would, your Brother had but half your
    Virtue !
Yet there remains a little Spark of Hope
That lights me to fome Comfort.   The Match is
    crofs'd ;
The Parties feparate ; and I again
May come to fee this Man that has betray'd me ;
And wound his Confcience for it: Home again
I will not go, whatever Fortune guides me ;
Tho' ev'ry Step I went, I trod upon
Dangers as fearful and as pale as Death.
No, no, *Henriquez* ; I will follow thee
Where there is Day.   Time may beget a Wonder.

Enters Servant.

O, are you come? What News?
    Serv None, but the worft. Your Father makes
mighty Offers yonder by a Cryer, to any One can
bring you home again.
    Viol. Art Thou corrupted?
    Serv. No.
    Viol. Wilt thou be honeft?
    Serv. I hope, you do not fear me.
    Viol. Indeed, I do not.   Thou haft an honeft Face ;
And fuch a Face, when it deceives, take heed,
Is curft of all Heav'n's Creatures.
    Serv. I'll hang firft.
    Viol. Heav'n blefs thee from that End! — I've heard
    a Man

D 3   Say

Say more than This; and yet that Man was falſe.
Thou'lt not be ſo, I hope.

Serv. By my Life, Miſtreſs, ———

Viol. Swear not; I credit Thee. But pry'thee tho',
Take Heed, thou doſt not fail: I do not doubt Thee:
Yet I have truſted ſuch a ſerious Face,
And been abuſed too.

Serv. If I fail your Truſt, ———

Viol. I do thee Wrong to hold thy Honeſty
At Diſtance thus: Thou ſhalt know all my Fortunes.
Get me a Shepherd's Habit.

Serv. Well; what elſe?

Viol. And wait me in the Evening, where I told thee;
There Thou ſhalt know my farther Ends. Take Heed—

Serv. D'ye fear me ſtill?

Viol. ——— ——— ——— No; This is only Counſel:
My Life and Death I have put equally
Into thy Hand: Let not Rewards, nor Hopes,
Be caſt into the Scale to turn thy Faith.

Be honeſt but for Virtue's ſake, that's all;
He, that has ſuch a Treaſure, cannot fall. [*Exeunt.*

The End of the Third Act.

ACT

ACT IV. SCENE I.

SCENE, *A Wide Plain, with a Prospect of Mountains at a Distance.*

Enter Master of the Flocks, three or four Shepherds, and Violante in Boy's Cloaths.

1 *Shep.* WELL, he's as sweet a Man, Heav'n comfort him! as ever these Eyes look'd on.

2 *Shep.* If he have a Mother, I believe, Neighbours, she's a Woe-woman for him at this Hour.

Mast. Why should he haunt these wild unpeopled Mountains,
Where nothing dwells but Hunger, and sharp Winds?

1 *Shep.* His Melancholy, Sir, that's the main Devil does it. Go to, I fear he has had too much foul Play offer'd him.

Mast. How gets he Meat?

2 *Shep.* Why, now and then he takes our Victuals from us, tho' we desire him to eat; and instead of a short Grace, beats us well and soundly, and then falls to.

Mast. Where lies He?

1 *Shep.* Ev'n where the Night o'ertakes him.

2 *Shep.* Now will I be hang'd, an' some fair-snouted skittish Woman, or other, be not at the End of this Madness.

1 *Shep.* Well, if he lodg'd within the Sound of us, I knew our Musick would allure him. How attentively he stood, and how he fix'd his Eyes, when your Boy sung his Love-Ditty. Oh, here he comes again.

Mast. Let him alone; he wonders strangely at us.

　　　　1 *Shep.*

1 *Shep.* Not a Word, Sirs, to croſs him, as you love your Shoulders.

2 *Shep.* He ſeems much diſturb'd: I believe the mad Fit is upon him.

Enters Julio.

Jul. Horſemanſhip!—— Hell—— Riding ſhall be abo-
    liſh'd:
Turn the barb'd Steed looſe to his native Wildneſs;
It is a Beaſt too noble to be made
The Property of Man's Baſeneſs.—— What a Letter
Wrote he to's Brother? What a Man was I?
Why, *Perſeus* did not know his Seat like me;
The *Parthian*, that rides ſwift without the Rein,
Match'd not my Grace and Firmneſs. ---Shall this Lord
Dye, when Men pray for him? Think you 'tis meet?

1 *Shep.* I don't know what to ſay: Neither I, nor
all the Confeſſors in *Spain*, can unriddle this wild Stuff.

Jul. I muſt to Court! be uſher'd into Grace,
By a large Liſt of Praiſes ready penn'd!
O Devil! What a venomous World is this,
When Commendations are the Baits to Ruin!
All theſe good Words were Gyves and Fetters, Sir,
To keep me bolted there: while the falſe Sender
Play'd out the Game of Treach'ry.—— Hold; come hi-
    ther;
You have an Aſpect, Sir, of wond'rous Wiſdom,
And, as it ſeems, are travell'd deep in Knowledge;
Have you e'er ſeen the *Phænix* of the Earth,
The Bird of Paradiſe?

2 *Shep.* ————In Troth, not I, Sir.

Jul. I have; and known her Haunts, and where ſhe
    built
Her ſpicy Neſt: 'till, like a credulous Fool,
I ſhew'd the Treaſure to a Friend in Truſt,
And he hath robb'd me of her.—— Truſt no Friend:
Keep thy Heart's Counſels cloſe. —— Haſt thou a Miſtreſs?
Give her not out in Words; nor let thy Pride
Be wanton to diſplay her Charms to View;

                        Love

Love is contagious: and a Breath of Praiſe,
Or a ſlight Glance, has kindled up its Flame,
And turn'd a Friend a Traytor.—— 'Tis in Proof;
And it has hurt my Brain.

    1 *Shep.* Marry, now there is ſome Moral in his Madneſs, and we may profit by it.

    Maſt. See, he grows cool, and penſive.
Go towards him, Boy, but do not look that way.

    Viol. Alas! I tremble ——

    Jul. ———————— Oh, my pretty Youth!
Come hither, Child; Did not your Song imply
Something of Love?

    1 *Shep.* Ha—ha— goes it there? Now if the Boy be witty, we ſhall trace ſomething.

    Viol. Yes, Sir, it was the Subjeƈt.

    Jul. Sit here then: Come, ſhake not, good pretty Soul,
Nor do not fear me; I'll not do thee Wrong.

    Viol. Why do you look ſo on me?

    Jul. ———— ———— I have Reaſons.
It puzzles my Philoſophy, to think
That the rude Blaſt, hot Sun, and daſhing Rains
Have made no fiercer War upon thy Youth;
Nor hurt the Bloom of that Vermilion Cheek.
You weep too, do you not?

    Viol. ———— Sometimes, I do.

    Jul. I weep ſometimes too. You're extremely young.

    Viol. Indeed, I've ſeen more Sorrows far than Years.

    Jul. Yet all theſe have not broken your Complexion.
You have a ſtrong Heart, and you are the happier.
I warrant, you're a very loving Woman.

    Viol. A Woman, Sir?— I fear, h'as found me out.
                       [*Aſide.*

    2 *Shep.* He takes the Boy for a Woman.— Mad, again!

    Jul. You've met ſome Diſappointment; ſome foul Play
Has croſs'd your Love.— I read it in your Face.

    Viol. You read a Truth then.

    Jul. ———— ———— Where can lie the Fault?
Is't in the Man, or ſome diſſembling Knave,
He put in Truſt? Ho! have I hit the Cauſe?

    Viol. You're not far off.

Jul.

Jul. This World is full of Coz'ners, very full;
Young Virgins muſt be wary in their Ways.
I've known a Duke's Son do as great a Knavery.
Will you be rul'd by me?
    Viol. ————————Yes.
    Jul. ————————Kill Yourſelf.
'Twill be a Terror to the Villain's Conſcience,
The longeſt Day he lives.
    Viol. ———————— By no Means.   What?
Commit Self-murther!
    Jul. ———— Yes; I'll have it ſo.
    1 *Shep.* I fear, his Fit is returning   Take heed of
all hands. —— Sir,—— do you want any thing?
    Jul. Thou ly'ſt; thou can'ſt not hurt me: I am proof
'Gainſt farther Wrongs. — Steal cloſe behind me, Lady.
I will avenge Thee.
    Viol. ————————Thank the Heav'ns, I'm free.
    Jul. O treach'rous, baſe *Henriquez!* have I caught
        thee?
    2 *Shep.* Help! help! good Neighbours; he will kill
        me elſe.   [Julio *ſeizes on the* Shepherd;
                                    Violante *runs out.*
    Jul. Here Thou ſhalt pay thy Heart-blood for the
        Wrongs
Thou'ſt heap'd upon this Head. Faith-breaker ! Villain!
I'll ſuck thy Life-blood.
    1 *Shep.* Good Sir, have Patience; this is no *Hen-*
        riquez.   [*They reſcue the* Shepherd.
    Jul. Well; let him ſlink to Court, and hide a Co-
        ward;
Not all his Father's Guards ſhall ſhield him there.
Or if he prove too ſtrong for Mortal Arm,
I will ſollicit ev'ry Saint in Heav'n
To lend me Vengeance. —— I'll about it ſtrait.——
The wrathful Elements ſhall wage this War;
Furies ſhall haunt him; Vultures gnaw his Heart;
And Nature pour forth all her Stores of Plagues,
To join in Puniſhment of Truſt betray'd. [*Exit* Julio.
    2 *Shep.* Go thy Ways, and a Vengeance go with
                                                        Thee!

Thee!——Pray, feel my Nofe; is it faft, Neighbours?

1 *Shep.* 'Tis as well as may be.

2 *Shep.* He pull'd at it, as he would have drag'd a
Bullock backward by the Tail.—— An't had been fome
Men's Nofe that I know, Neighbours, who knows
where it had been now? He has given me fuch a de-
vilifh Dafh o'er the Mouth, that I feel, I fhall never
whiftle to my Sheep again: Then they'll make Holy-day.

1 *Shep.* Come, fhall we go? for, I fear, if the Youth
return, our fecond Courfe will be much more againft
our Stomachs.

Maft. Walk you afore; I will but give my Boy
Some fhort Inftructions, and I'll follow ftrait.
We'll crafh a Cup together.

1 *Shep.* Pray, do not linger.

Maft. I will not, Sirs; ——This muft not be a Boy;
His Voice, Mein, Gefture, ev'ry Thing he does,
Savour of foft and female Delicacy.
He but puts on this Seeming, and his Garb
Speaks him of fuch a Rank, as well perfwades me,
He plays the Swain, rather to cloak fome Purpofe,
Than forced to't by a Need: I've waited long
To mark the End he has in his Difguife;
But am not perfect in't. The Madman's Coil
Has driv'n him fhaking hence. Thefe Fears betray him.
If he prove right, I'm happy. O, he's here.

Enters Violante.

Come hither, Boy; where did you leave the Flock,
Child?

Viol. Grazing below, Sir. — What does he mean,
to ftroke One o'the Cheek fo? I hope, I'm not betray'd.

Maft. Have you learnt the Whiftle yet, and when
to Fold?
And how to make the Dog bring in the Strayers?

Viol. Time, Sir, will furnifh me with all thefe Rules;
My Will is able, but my Knowledge weak, Sir.

Maft. That's a good Child: Why doft thou blufh,
my Boy?

'Tis

'Tis certainly a Woman. [*Aſide.*] Speak, my Boy.

Viol. Heav'n! how I tremble. — 'Tis unuſual to me
To find ſuch Kindneſs at a Maſter's Hand,
That am a poor Boy, ev'ry way unable,
Unleſs it be in Pray'rs, to merit it.
Beſides, I've often heard old People ſay,
Too much Indulgence makes Boys rude and ſawcy.

Maſt. Are you ſo cunning!——

Viol. —————————How his Eyesſhake Fire,
And meaſure ev'ry Piece of Youth about me! [*Aſide.*
The Ewes want Water, Sir: Shall I go drive 'em
Down to the Ciſterns? Shall I make haſte, Sir?
'Would I were five Miles from him—— How he gripes
 me! [*Aſide.*

Maſt. Come, come, all this is not ſufficient, Child,
To make a Fool of me.—— This is a fine Hand,
A delicate fine Hand,—— Never change Colour;
You underſtand me,—and a Woman's Hand.

Viol. You're ſtrangely out: Yet if I were a Woman,
I know, you are ſo honeſt and ſo good,
That tho' I wore Diſguiſes for ſome Ends,
You would not wrong me.——

Maſt. —————Come, you're made for Love;
Will you comply? I'm madder with this Talk.
There's Nothing you can ſay, can take my Edge off.

Viol. Oh, do but quench theſe foul Affectionsin you,
That, like baſe Thieves, have rob'd you of your Reaſon,
And I will be a Woman; and begin
So ſad a Story, that if there be aught
Of humane in you, or a Soul that's gentle,
You cannot chuſe but pity my loſt Youth.

Maſt. No Stories now.——

Viol. —————————Kill me directly, Sir;
As vou have any Goodneſs, take my Life.

Rod. within. Hoa! Shepherd, will you hear, Sir?

Maſt. What bawling Rogue is that, i'th' Devil's
 Name?

Viol. Bleſſings upon him, whatſoe'er he be! [*Runs out.*
                                                    Enters

Enters Roderick.

Rod. Good Even, my Friend; I thought, you all had been afleep in this Country.

Maft. You had lied then; for you were waking, when you thought fo.

Rod. I thank you, Sir.

Maft I pray, be cover'd; 'tis not fo much worth, Sir.

Rod. Was that thy Boy ran crying?

Maft. Yes; what then?

Rod Why doft thou beat him fo?

Maft. To make him grow.

Rod. A pretty Med'cine! Thou can'ft not tell me the Way to the next Nunnery?———

Maft. How do you know That? — Yes, I can tell you; but the Queftion is, whether I will or no; and, indeed, I will not. Fare you well   [*Exit* Mafter.

Rod What a brute Fellow's this! Are they all thus? My Brother *Henriquez* tells me by his Letters, The Miftrefs of his Soul not far from hence Hath taken Sanctuary: from which he prays My Aid to bring her back.—From what *Camillo* Hinted, I wear fome Doubts.—— Here 'tis appointed That we fhould meet; it muft be here; 'tis fo. He comes.

Enters Henriquez.

Now, Brother, what's this poft-hafte Bufinefs You hurry me about? ——- Some wenching Matter—

Henr. My Letter told you, Sir.

Rod. 'Tis true, it tells me, that you've loft a Miftrefs Whom your Heart bleeds for; but the Means to win her From her clofe Life, I take it, is not mention d. You're ever in thefe Troubles.———

Henr. ———————Noble Brother, I own, I have too freely giv'n a Scope

To

To Youth's intemp'rate Heat, and rafh Defires:
But think not, that I would engage your Virtues
To any Caufe, wherein my conftant Heart
Attended not my Eye. 'Till now my Paffions
Reign'd in my Blood; ne'er pierc'd into my Mind;
But I'm a Convert grown to pureft Thoughts:
And muft in Anguifh fpend my Days to come,
If I poffefs not her: So much I love.

   Rod. The Means? —She's in a Cloyfter, is fhe not?
Within whofe Walls to enter as We are,
Will never be: Few Men, but Fryars, come there;
Which We fhall never make.

   Henr. ———— If That would do it,
I would make Any thing.

   Rod. ———————— Are you fo hot?
I ll ferve him, be it but to fave his Honour.   [*Afide.*
To feign a Corpfe —— By th' Mafs, it fhall be fo.
We muft pretend, we do tranfport a Body
As 'twere to's Funeral: and coming late by,
Crave a Night's Leave to reft the Herfe i'th' Convent.
That be our Courfe; for to fuch Charity
Strict Zeal and Cuftom of the Houfe give Way.

   Henr. And, opportune, a vacant Herfe pafs'd by
From Rites but new perform'd: This for a Price
We'll hire, to put our Scheme in Act. Ho! *Gerald*—
   [*Enter* Gerald, *whom* Henriquez *whifpers; then* Ge-
   rald *goes out.*

   Rod. When we're once lodg'd, the Means of her
      Conveyance,
By fafe and fecret Force, with Eafe we'll compafs.
But, Brother, know my Terms. — If that your Miftrefs
Will to the World come back, and fhe appear
An Object worthy in our Father's Eye,
Wooe her, and win her; but if his Confent
Keep not Pace with your Purpofe ——

   Henr. Doubt it not.
I've look'd not with a common Eye; but chofe
A noble Virgin, who to make her fo,

Has

Has all the Gifts of Heav'n and Earth upon her.
If ever Woman yet could be an Angel,
She is the neareft.
    Rhod. ———— Well; a Lover's Praife
Feafts not a Common Ear. ———— Now to our Plot;
We fhall bring Night in with Us.   [*Exeunt*.

S C E N E II.

Enter Julio, *and Two Gentlemen.*

    Gent. Good Sir, compofe yourfelf.
    Jul. ——————————— O *Leonora,*
That Heav'n had made Thee ftronger than a Woman,
How happy had I been!
    Gent. —————— He's calm again:
I'll take this Interval to work upon Him.
Thefe wild and folitary Places, Sir,
But feed your Pain; let better Reafon guide you;
And quit this forlorne State, that yields no Comfort.
                       [*Lute founds within*
    Jul. Ha! hark, a Sound from Heav'n! Do you hear
      Nothing?
    Gent. Yes, Sir; the Touch of fome fweet Inftrument:
Here's no Inhabitant.
    Jul. ————— No, no, the better.
    Gent. This is a ftrange Place to hear Mufick in.
    Jul. I'm often vifited with thefe fweet Airs.
The Spirit of fome haplefs Man that dy'd,
And left his Love hid in a faithlefs Woman,
Sure haunts thefe Mountains.   [*Violante fings within.*
     Fond Echo*! forego thy light Strain,*
       And heedfully hear a loft Maid;
     Go, tell the falfe Ear of the Swain
       How deeply his Vows have betray'd.
     Go, tell him, what Sorrows I bear;
       See, yet if his Heart feel my Woe:
    'Tis now he muft heal my Defpair,
       Or Death will make Pity too flow.

                                 Gent.

Gent. See, how his Soul ſtrives in him! This ſad Strain
Has ſearch'd him to the Heart.

Jul. Excellent Sorrow!
You never lov'd?

Gent. No.

Jul. ——— Peace; and learn to grieve then.

[*Violante ſings within.*

> *Go, tell him, what Sorrows I bear;*
> *See, yet if his Heart feel my Woe:*
> *'Tis now he muſt heal my Deſpair,*
> *Or Death will make Pity too ſlow.*

Is not this heav'nly?

Gent. I never heard the Like, Sir.

Jul. I'll tell you, my good Friends; but pray, ſay Nothing;
I'm ſtrangely touch'd with This..The heav'nly Sound
Diffuſes a ſweet Peace thro' all my Soul.
But yet I wonder, what new, ſad, Companion
Grief has brought hither to out bid my Sorrows.
Stand off, ſtand off, ſtand off——Friends, it appears.

Enters Violante.

Viol. How much more grateful are theſe craggy Mountains,
And theſe wild Trees, than things of nobler Natures,
For Theſe receive my Plaints, and mourn again
In many Echoes to Me. All good People
Are faln aſleep for ever. None are left,
That have the Senſe, and Touch of Tenderneſs
For Virtue's ſake: No, ſcarce their Memory:
From whom I may expect Counſel in Fears,
Eaſe to Complainings, or Redreſs of Wrongs.

Jul. This is a moving Sorrow, but ſay nothing.

Viol. What Dangers have I run, and to what Inſults
Expos'd this Ruin of my ſelf? Oh! Miſchief
On that Soul-ſpotted Hind, my vicious Maſter!

Who

Who would have thought, that such poor Worms as
   They,
(Whose best Feed is coarse Bread; whose Bev'rage,
   Water;)
Should have so much rank Blood? I shake all over,
And blush to think what had become of me,
If that good Man had not reliev'd me from him.

Jul. Since she is not *Leonora*, she is heav'nly.
When she speaks next, listen as seriously,
As Women do that have their Loves at Sea,
What Wind blows ev'ry Morning. ———

Viol. I cannot get this false Man's Memory
Out of my Mind. You Maidens, that shall live
To hear my mournful Tale, when I am Ashes,
Be wise; and to an Oath no more give Credit,
To Tears, to Vows, (false Both!) or any Thing
A Man shall promise, than to Clouds, that now
Bear such a pleasing Shape, and now are nothing.
For they will cozen, (if They may be cozen'd,)
The very Gods they worship. ——— Valour, Justice,
Discretion, Honesty, and all they covet,
To make them seeming Saints, are but the Wiles
By which these *Syrens* lure us to Destruction.

Jul. Do not you weep now? I could drop myself
Into a Fountain for her

Gent. She weeps extremely.

Jul. ——————————— Let her weep; 'tis well:
Her Heart will break else. Great Sorrows live in Tears.

Viol. O false *Henriquez!* ———

Jul. ——————— Ha!

Viol. ——————— And Oh, thou Fool,
Forsaken *Violante!* whose Belief
And childish Love have made Thee so ——— go, dye;
For there is nothing left Thee now to look for,
That can bring Comfort, but a quiet Grave.
There all the Miseries I long have felt,
And Those to come, shall sweetly sleep together.
Fortune may guide that false *Henriquez* hither,
To weep Repentance o'er my pale, dead Coarse,

          And

And cheer my wand'ring Spirit with thofe lov'd Obfe-
    quies.   [*Going.*

Jul. Stay, Lady, ftay: Can it be poffible,
That you are *Violante?*

Viol. —————— That loft Name,
Spoken by One, that needs muft know my Fortunes,
Has taken much Fear from me. Who are you, Sir?
For, fure, I am that hopelefs *Violante.*

Jul. And I, as far from any earthly Comfort
That I know yet, the much-wrong'd *Julio!*

Viol. ————————————— *Julio!*

Jul. I once was thought fo. ——— If the curft
    Henriquez
Had Pow'r to change you to a Boy, why, Lady,
Should not that Mifchief make me any thing,
That have an equal Share in all the Miferies
His Crimes have flung upon Us?

Viol. ——— ——————— Well I know it:
And pardon Me, I could not know your Virtues,
Before your Griefs. Methought, when laft we met,
The Accent of your Voice ftruck on my Ear
Like fomething I had known, but Floods of Sorrow
Drown'd the Remembrance. If you'll pleafe to fit,
(Since I have found a fuff'ring true Companion,)
And give me Hearing, I will tell you fomething
Of *Leonora*, that may comfort you.

Jul. Bleffing upon Thee! Henceforth, I proteft
Never to leave Thee, if Heav'n fay *Amen.*
But, foft! let's fhift our Ground, guide our fad Steps
To fome remoter Gloom, where, undifturb'd,
We may compare our Woes; dwell on the Tale
Of mutual Injuries, 'till our Eyes run o'er,
And we infect each other, with frefh Sorrows. ——
Talk'd you of Comfort? 'Tis the Food of Fools,
And We will None on't; but indulge Defpair:
So, worn with Griefs, ftcal to the Cave of Death,
And in a Sigh give up our lateft Breath.   [*Exeunt.*

The End of the Fourth Act.

                                             ACT

ACT V. SCENE I.

SCENE, *The Prospect of the Moun-*
tains continued.

Enter Roderick, Leonora *veil'd*, Henriquez, *Atten-*
dants as Mourners.

Rod. REST certain, Lady, Nothing ſhall betide
you,
But fair, and noble Uſage. Pardon me,
That hitherto a Courſe of Violence
Has ſnatch'd you from that Seat of Contemplation
To which you gave your After-Life.
   Leon. Where am I ?
   Rod. Not in the Nunnery; never bluſh, nor trem-
ble;
Your Honour has as fair a Guard, as when
Within a Cloyſter. Know then, what is done,
(Which, I preſume, you underſtand not truly,)
Has this Uſe, to preſerve the Life of One
Dying for Love of You : my Brother, and your
   Friend :
Under which Colour we deſir'd to reſt
Our Herſe one Night within your hallow'd Walls,
Where we ſurpriz'd you.
   Leon. ———— Are you that Lord *Roderick,*
So ſpoken of for Virtue, and fair Life,
And dare you loſe theſe to be Advocate
For ſuch a Brother, ſuch a ſinful Brother,
Such

Such an unfaithful, treacherous, brutal Brother?

Rod. This is a fearful Charge. ———

                     [*Looks at* Henriquez.

Leon. ——————If you would have me

Think, you ftill bear Refpect for Virtue's Name;

As you would wifh, your Daughters, thus diftrefs'd,

Might find a Guard, protect me from *Henriquez* ;

And I am happy.

    Rod. ——— Come, Sir, make your Anfwer ;

For as I have a Soul, I am afham'd on't.

    Henr. O *Leonora*, fee! thus felf-condemn'd,

I throw me at your Feet, and fue for Mercy.

If I have err'd, impute it to my Love;

The Tyrant God that bows us to his Sway,

Rebellious to the Laws of reas'ning Men;

That will not have his Votaries Actions fcann'd,

But calls it Juftice, when we moft obey him.

He but commanded, what your Eyes infpir'd;

Whofe facred Beams, darted into my Soul,

Have purg'd the Manfion from impure Defires,

And kindled in my Heart a Veftal's Flame.

    Leon. Rife, rife, my Lord; this well-diffembled Paffion

Has gain'd you nothing but a deeper Hate.

Should I imagine, he can truly love me,

That, like a Villain, murthers my Defires?

Or fhould I drink that Wine, and think it Cordial,

When I fee Poyfon in't?

    Rod. ——————— Draw this way, Lady;

I am not perfect in your Story yet;

But fee you've had fome Wrongs, that want Redrefs.

Only you muft have Patience to go with us

To yon fmall Lodge, which meets the Sight from hence,

Where your Diftrefs fhall find the due Refpect:

'Till when, your Griefs fhall govern me as much,

As Nearnefs and Affection to my Brother.

Call my Attendants yours; and ufe them freely;

                             For

For as I am a Gentleman, no Pow'r,
Above your own Will, fhall come near your Perfon.
   [*As they are going out,* Violante *enters, and plucks*
      Roderick *by the Sleeve; the reſt go out.*]
   Viol. Your Ear a Moment: Scorn not my tender
      Youth.
   Roder. Look to the Lady there. —— I follow ſtrait.
What ails this Boy? Why doſt thou fingle me?
   Viol. The due Obfervance of your noble Virtue,
Vow'd to this mourning Virgin, makes me bold
To give it more Employment.
   Rod. —— —— Art not Thou
The furly Shepherd's Boy, that, when I call'd
To know the Way, ran crying by me?
   Viol. Yes, Sir.
And I thank Heav'n and you for helping me.
   Rod. How did I help thee, Boy?
   Viol. I do but feem fo, Sir ; and am indeed
A Woman; one your Brother once has lov'd ;
Or, Heav'n forgive him elfe, he ly'd extremely.
   Rod. Weep not, good Maid; O this licentious
      Brother!
But how came you a Wand'rer on thefe Mountains?
   Viol. That, as we pafs, an't pleafe you, I'll difcover.
I will affure you, Sir, thefe barren Mountains
Hold many Wonders of your Brother's making.
Here wanders haplefs *Julio,* worthy Man!
Befides himfelf with Wrongs——
   Rod. That once again ——
   Viol. Sir, I faid, *Julio.*—— Sleep weigh'd down his
      Eyelids,
Oppreſs'd with Watching, juſt as you approach'd us.
   Rod. O Brother! We fhall found the Depths of
      Falfhood.
If this be true, no more but guide me to him:
I hope, a fair End will fucceed all yet.
If it be He, by your Leave, gentle Brother,
I'll fee him ferv'd firſt. —— Maid, you have o'erjoy'd me.
          E 3   Thou

Thou fhalt have Right too: Make thy fair Appeal
To the good Duke, and doubt not but thy Tears
Shall be repaid with Intereft from his Juftice.
Lead me to *Julio*. [*Exeunt*.

SCENE II. *An Apartment in the Lodge*.

Enter Duke, Don Bernard, *and* Camillo.

Cam. Ay, then your Grace had had a Son more;
He, a Daughter; and I, an Heir: But let it be as 'tis,
I cannot mend it; one way or other, I fhall rub it o-
ver, with rubbing to my Grave, and there's an End on't.

Duke. Our Sorrows cannot help us, Gentlemen.

Cam. Hang me, Sir, if I fhed one Tear more. By
Jove, I've wept fo long, I'm as blind as Juftice. When
I come to fee my Hawks (which I held a Toy next to
my Son;) if they be but Houfe-high, I muft ftand
aiming at them like a Gunner.

Duke. Why, he mourns like a Man. *Don Bernard,*
you
Are ftill like *April*, full of Show'rs and Dews:
And yet I blame you not: for I myfelf
Feel the felf-fame Affections. —— Let them go;
They're difobedient Children.

D. Bern. ———————— Ay, my Lord;
Yet they may turn again.

Cam. Let them e'en have their Swing: they're young
and wanton; the next Storm we fhall have them gallop homeward, whining as Pigs do in the Wind.

D. Bern Would I had my Daughter any way.

Cam. Would'ft thou have her with Bearn, Man, tell
me that?

D. Bern. I care not, if an honeft Father got it.

Cam. You might have had her fo in this good Time,
Had my Son had her: Now you may go feek
Your Fool to ftop a Gap with.

Duke

Duke. You fay, that *Rod'rick* charg'd you here fhould
  wait him:
He has o'erflip'd the Time, at which his Letters
Of Speed requeft that I fhould alfo meet him.
I fear, fome bad Event is ufher'd in
By this Delay: —— How now?

     Enters Gentleman.

  Gent. —— So pleafe your Grace,
Lord *Rod'rick* makes Approach.
  Duke. —— I thank thee, Fellow,
For thy fo timely News: Comes he alone?
  Gent. No, Sir, attended well: and in his Train
Follows a Herfe with all due Rites of Mourning.
         [*Exit Gent.*

  Duke. Heav'n fend, *Henriquez* live!
  Cam. ——'Tis my poor *Julio.* ——

     Enters Roderick, *haftily.*

  Duke. O welcome, welcome,
Welcome, good *Rod'rick!* Say, what News?
  Cam. Do you bring Joy or Grief, my Lord? For me,
Come what can come, I'll live a Month or two
If the Gout pleafe; curfe my Phyfician once more,
And then, —— ——

     Under this Stone
     Lies Sev'nty One.

  Rod. Signior, you do exprefs a manly Patience.
My noble Father, fomething I have brought
To eafe your Sorrows: My Endeavours have not
Been altogether barren in my Journey.
  Duke. It comes at need, Boy; but I hop'd it from
  thee.

        Enter

Enter Leonora *veil'd*, Henriquez *behind, and Attendants.*

Rod. The Company I bring, will bear me Witnels
The buliest of my Time has been employ'd
On this good Task. *Don Bernard* finds beneath
This Veil his Daughter: You, my Royal Father,
Behind that Lady find a wand'ring Son.
How I met with them, and how brought them hither,
More Leifure mult unfold.
   Henr. —————————— My Father here!
And *Julio*'s! O Confufion!—— Low as Earth
I bow me for your Pardon.   [*To the Duke.*
   D. Bern. O my Girl!
Thou bring'lt new Life. ——   [*Embraces* Leonora.
   Duke. And you, my Son, reltore me [*To* Roderick.
One Comfort here that has been milling long.
I hope, thy Follies thou halt left abroad. [*To* Henriq.
   Cam. Ay, ay; you've all Comforts but I; you have
ruin'd me, kill'd my poor Boy; cheated and ruin'd him;
and I have no Comfort.
   Rod. Be patient, Signior; Time may guide my
     Hand.
To work you Comfort too.
   Cam. I thank your Lordfhip ;
'Would Grandfire Time had been fo kind to 've done it;
We might have joy'd together like good Fellows.
But he's fo full of Bufinefs, good Old Man,
'Tis Wonder, he could do the Good he has done.
   D. Bern. Nay, Child, be comforted. Thefe Tears
diltraᴆ me.
   Duke. Hear your good Father, Lady.
   Leon. —— Willingly.
   Duke. The Voice of Parents is the Voice of Gods:
For to their Children they are Heav'n's Lieutenants:
Made Fathers, not for common Ufes meerly
Of Procreation; (Bealts and Birds would.be

As

As noble then as we are) but to fteer
The wanton Freight of Youth thro' Storms and Dan-
gers,
Which with full Sails they bear upon: and ftreighten
The moral Line of Life, they bend fo often.
For Thefe are We made Fathers; and for Thefe,
May challenge Duty on our Children's Part.
Obedience is the Sacrifice of Angels,
Whofe Form you carry.

    D. Bern. Hear the Duke, good Wench.
    Leon. I do moft heedfully. My gracious Lord,
                                 [*To the Duke.*

Let me be fo unmanner d to requeft,
He would not farther prefs me with Perfuafions
O'th' inftant Hour: but have the gentle Patience
To bury this keen Suit, 'till I fhake Hands
With my old Sorrows, ————
    Cam. ———— Why doft look at me?
Alas! I cannot help thee.
    Leon. ———————— And but weep
A Farewell to my murther'd *Julio*, ————
    Cam. Blefling be with thy Soul, whene'er it leaves
    Thee!
    Leon. For fuch fad Rites muft be perform'd, my
    Lord,
E'er I can love again. Maids, that have lov'd,
If they be worth that noble Teftimony,
Wear their Loves here, my Lord; here, in their
    Hearts;
Deep, deep within; not in their Eyes, or Accents;
Such may be flip'd away; or with two Tears
Wafh'd out of all Remembrance: Mine, no Phyfick,
But Time, or Death, can cure.
    Henr. You make your own Conditions, and I feal
    them
Thus on your virtuous Hand.   [*Afide.*
    Cam. Well, Wench, thy Equal
Shall not be found in hafte; I give thee That:

                                 Thou

Thou art a right one, ev'ry Inch —— Thy Father
(For, without Doubt, that Snuff never begot Thee,)
Was some choice Fellow, some true Gentleman;
I give thy Mother Thanks for't —— there's no Harm
 done. ——

Would I were young again, and had but thee,
A good Horse under me, and a good Sword,
And thus much for Inheritance. ——

    [*Violante offers, once or twice, to shew*
      herself, but goes back.

 Duke. What Boy's That,
Has offer'd twice or thrice to break upon us?
I've noted him, and still he falls back fearful.
 Rod. A little Boy, Sir, like a Shepherd?
 Duke. Yes.
 Rod. 'Tis your Page, Brother; —— One that
 was so, late.
 Henr. My Page! What Page?
 Rod. —— Ev'n so he says, your Page;
And more, and worse, you stole him from his Friends,
And promis'd him Preferment.
 Henr. I, Preferment!
 Rod. And on some slight Occasion let him slip
Here on these Mountains, where he had been starv'd,
Had not my People found him, as we travell'd.
This was not handsome, Brother.
 Henr. —— You are merry.
 Rod. You'll find it sober Truth.
 Duke. —— If so, 'tis ill.
 Henr. 'Tis Fiction all, Sir; ——Brother, you must
 please
To look some other Fool to put these Tricks on;
They are too obvious: —— Please your Grace, give
 Leave
T' admit the Boy; If he know me, and say,
I stole him from his Friends, and cast him off,
Know me no more. ——Brother, pray do not wrong
 me.

           Enters

Enters Violante.

Rod. Here is the Boy. If he deny this to you,
Then I have wrong'd you.
 Duke. ——— Hear me; What's thy Name, Boy?
 Viol. Florio, an't like your Grace.
 Duke. ———————- A pretty Child.
Where waſt thou born?
 Viol. ——— On t'other Side the Mountains.
 Duke. What are thy Friends?
 Viol. ——————— A Father, Sir; but poor.
 Duke. How cameſt thou hither? how, to leave thy
  Father?
 Viol. That noble Gentleman pleas'd once to like
  me,   [*Pointing to* Henriquez.
And, not to lye, ſo much to doat upon me,
That with his Promiſes he won my Youth,
And Duty, from my Father: Him I follow'd.
 Rod. How ſay you now, Brother?
 Cam. ——— Ay, my Lord, how ſay You?
 Hen. As I have Life and Soul, 'tis all a Trick, Sir.
I never ſaw the Boy before.
 Viol. ——————— O Sir,
Call not your Soul to witneſs in a Wrong:
And 'tis not noble in you, to deſpiſe
What you have made thus. If I lye, let Juſtice
Turn all her Rods upon me.
 Duke. ——————— Fye, *Henriquez*;
There is no Trace of Cunning in this Boy.
 Cam. A good Boy! ——— Be not fearful: Speak thy
  Mind, Child.
Nature, ſure, meant thou ſhould'ſt have been a Wench;
And then't had been no Marvel he had bobb'd thee.
 Duke. Why did he put thee from him?
 Viol. ——————— That to me
Is yet unknown, Sir; for my Faith, he could not;
I never did deceive him: for my Service,

           He

He had no juft Caufe; what my Youth was able,
My Will ftill put in Act, to pleafe my Mafter:
I cannot fteal; therefore that can be nothing
To my Undoing: no, nor lye; my Breeding,
Tho' it be plain, is honeft.

Duke. —————————— Weep not, Child.

Cam. This Lord has abufed Men, Women, and
Children already: What farther Plot he has, the Devil
knows.

Duke. If thou can'ft bring a Witnefs of thy Wrong,
(Elfe it would be Injuftice to believe thee,
He having fworn againft it;) thou fhalt have,
I bind it with my Honour, Satisfaction
To thine own Wifhes.

Viol. —————————— I defire no more, Sir.
I have a Witnefs, and a noble one,
For Truth and Honefty.

Rod. —————Go, bring him hither. [*Exit* Violante

Henr. This lying Boy will take him to his Heels,
And leave me flander'd.

Rod. —————————— No; I'll be his Voucher.

Henr. Nay then 'tis plain, this is Confederacy.

Rod. That he has been an Agent in your Service,
Appears from this. Here is a Letter, Brother,
(Produc'd, perforce, to give him Credit with me;)
The Writing, yours; the Matter, Love; for fo,
He fays, he can explain it.

Cam. —————————————— Then, belike,
A young He-bawd.

Henr. —————————This Forgery confounds me!

Duke. Read it, *Roderick.*

Rod. Reads.] *Our Prudence fhould now teach us to*
               forget, what our Indifcretion has com-
               mitted. I have already made one Step
               towards this Wifdom ————

Henr. Hold, Sir.—— My very Words to *Violante!*
                                        [*Afide.*

Duke. Go on.

                                        Henr.

Henr —— My gracious Father, give me Pardon;
I do confeſs, I ſome ſuch Letter wrote
(The Purport all too trivial for your Ear,)
But how it reach'd this young Diſſembler's Hands,
Is what I cannot ſolve. For on my Soul,
And by the Honours of my Birth and Houſe,
The Minion's Face 'till now I never ſaw.
 Rod. Run not too far in Debt on Proteſtation.——
Why ſhould you do a Child this Wrong?
 Henr. —————— —————— —— Go to;
Your Friendſhips paſt warrant not this Abuſe:
If you provoke me thus, I ſhall forget
What you are to me. This is a meer Practice,
And Villany to draw me into Scandal.
 Rod. No more; you are a Boy. —— Here comes a
  Witneſs,
Shall prove you ſo: No more.————

  Enter Julio, *diſguis'd;* Violante, *as a Woman.*

 Henr. —————— ———— Another Raſcal!
 Duke. Hold : ——
 Henr. Ha!   [*Seeing* Violante.
 Duke. What's here?
 Henr. By all my Sins, the injur'd *Violante.* [*Aſide.*
 Rod. Now, Sir, whoſe Practice breaks?
 Cam ———— —— Is this a Page? [*To* Henr.
 Rod. One that has done him Service,
And he has paid her for't; but broke his Covenant.
 Viol. My Lord, I come not now to wound your
  Spirit.
Your pure Affection dead, which firſt betray'd me,
My Claim dye with it! Only let me not
Shrink to the Grave with Infamy upon me:
Protect my Virtue, tho' it hurt your Faith;
And my laſt Breath ſhall ſpeak *Henriquez* noble.
 Henr. What a fierce Conflict Shame, and wounded
  Honour,

            Raiſe

Raife in my Breaft! — but Honour fhall o'ercome.—
She looks as beauteous, and as innocent,
As when I wrong'd her. — Virtuous *Violante*!
Too good for me! dare you ftill love a Man,
So faithlefs as I am?— I know you love me.
Thus, thus, and thus, I print my vow'd Repentance :
Let all Men read it here.— My gracious Father,
Forgive, and make me rich with your Confent,
This is my Wife; no other would I chufe,
Were fhe a Queen.

   Cam. Here's a new Change. *Bernard* looks dull upon't.

   Henr. And fair *Leonora*, from whofe Virgin Arms
I forc'd my wrong'd Friend *Julio*, O forgive me.
Take home your holy Vows, and let him have 'em
That has deferv'd them. O that he were here!
That I might own the Bafenefs of my Wrong,
And purpos'd Recompence. My *Violante*,
You muft again be widow'd : for I vow
A ceafelefs Pilgrimage, ne'er to know Joy,
'Till I can give it to the injur'd *Julio*.

   Cam. This almoft melts me:—— But my poor loft
   Boy——

   Rod. I'll ftop that Voyage, Brother.—Gentle Lady,
What think you of this honeft Man?

   Leon. Alas!
My Thoughts, my Lord, were all employ'd within!
He has a Face makes me remember fomething
I have thought well of; how he looks upon me!
Poor Man, he weeps. —Ha! ftay; it cannot be —
He has his Eye, his Features, Shape, and Gefture.—
'Would, he would fpeak.

   Jul. —— *Leonora*, —   [*Throws off his Difguife.*
   Leon. —————— Yes, 'tis He.
O Ecftacy of Joy!——   [*They embrace.*

   Cam. Now, what's the Matter?

   Rod. Let 'em alone; they're almoft ftarv'd for
   Kiffes.

   Cam. Stand forty Foot off; no Man trouble 'em.

                         Much

Much Good may't do your Hearts!—What is he, Lord,
What is he?

Rod. A certain Son of yours.

Cam.————— The Devil he is.

Rod. If he be the Devil, that Devil muſt call you
Father.

    Cam. By your Leave a little, ho, —Are you my *Julio?*

Jul. My Duty tells me ſo, Sir,
Still on my Knees. — But Love engroſs'd me all;
O *Leonora,* do I once more hold thee?

    Cam. Nay, to't again: I will not hinder you a Kiſs,
    'Tis he———   [*Leaps.*

    Leon. The righteous Pow'rs at length have crown'd
    our Loves.

Think, *Julio,* from the Storm that's now o'erblown,
Tho' ſour Affliction combat Hope awhile,
When Lovers ſwear true Faith, the liſt'ning Angels
Stand on the golden Battlements of Heav'n,
And waſt their Vows to the Eternal Throne.
Such were our Vows, and ſo are they repaid.

    Duke. E en as you are, we'll join your Hands to-
    gether.

A Providence above our Pow'r rules all.
Ask him Forgiveneſs, Boy.   [*To* Henriquez.

    Jul. ——— He has it, Sir:
The Fault was Love's, not his.

    Henr. ———— Brave, gen'rous *Julio!*
I knew thy Nobleneſs of old, and priz'd it,
'Till Paſſiom made me blind —Once more, my Friend,
Share in a Heart, that ne'er ſhall wrong thee more.
And, Brother,

    Rod. ———— This Embrace cuts off Excuſes.

    Duke. I muſt, in part, repair my Son's Offence:
At your beſt Leiſure, *Julio,* know our Court.
And, *Violante,* (for I know you now;)
I have a Debt to pay: Your good old Father,
Once, when I chas'd the Boar, preſerv'd my Life:
For that good Deed, and for your Virtue's Sake,

Tho' your Defcent be low, call me your Father.
A Match drawn out of Honefty, and Goodnefs,
Is Pedigree enough. ——— Are you all pleas'd?

[*Gives her to* Henriquez.

Camil. All.
Henr. } ——— All, Sir,
D. Bern. }
Jul. All.
Duke. And I not leaft. We'll now return to Court :
(And that fhort Travel, and your Loves compleated,
Shall, as I truft, for Life reftrain thefe Wand'rings.)
There, the Solemnity, and Grace, I'll do
Your fev'ral Nuptials, fhall approve my Joy ;
And make griev'd Lovers, that your Story read,
Wifh, true Love's Wand'rings may like yours fucceed.

[*Curtain falls.*

F I N I S.